IF

overland supersonic flight is permitted 500,-000,000 persons in America, Europe and Asia may be jolted every hour, day and night, by sonic booms from hit and run S/S/Ts. People working, relaxing, sleeping will be banged repeatedly, without apology. Homes, hospitals, schools and churches will no longer be havens from the bustle of modern life. In the U.S.A. alone the damage to glass and plaster may amount to $3 million per day. Aviation, instead of being man's servant, would be his scourge.

Why should the public—95% of whose members would never fly in an S/S/T—be forced to provide billions of dollars for an inefficient, unnecessary plane that could destroy peace and quiet throughout much of the civilized world?

In the S/S/T AND SONIC BOOM HANDBOOK William A. Shurcliff presents the arguments against the super-sonic transport which will affect every living person—*unless the public demands a halt right now.*

BALLANTINE BOOKS
in cooperation with
THE SIERRA CLUB

THE POPULATION BOMB, Dr. Paul R. Ehrlich $.95

Overpopulation is now the dominant problem in all our personal, national and international planning. Dr. Paul R. Ehrlich, Professor of Biology and Director of Graduate Study for the Department of Biological Sciences, Stanford University, describes the dimensions of the crisis in all its aspects and provides a realistic evaluation of the remaining options.

VOICES FOR THE WILDERNESS,
    edited by William Schwartz $1.25

The key papers that have shaped the growing movement to preserve the Wilderness. William O. Douglas, Ashley Montagu, David Brower, Wallace Stegner, Stewart L. Udall and Joseph Wood Krutch are among the contributors to this comprehensive anthology from the Sierra Club Wilderness Conferences.

ALMOST ANCESTORS: The First Californians
Theodora Kroeber and Robert F. Heizer $3.95

The author of *Ishi in Two Worlds* joins the photographer Robert F. Heizer in presenting this original collection of 100 photographs of the Indians of California. The pictures, dating back to 1851 and collected from museums and private sources, are beautifully reproduced in the large format 8½″ x 11″ size and printed in two tones of black. *A Sierra Club/ Ballantine Book in the Exhibit Format series.*

For a complete list of Ballantine Books, or to order by mail, write to: Dept. CS, Ballantine Books, 36 West 20th Street, New York, N.Y. 10003.

S/S/T
AND
SONIC BOOM
HANDBOOK

William A. Shurcliff

BALLANTINE BOOKS   •   NEW YORK

An Intext Publisher

BALLANTINE BOOKS, INC.
101 Fifth Avenue, New York, New York 10003

Contents

"You and your newly formed organization are making an invaluable contribution. I am grateful to you for sharing the findings of your research effort with me."

SENATOR WILLIAM PROXMIRE (D. Wisc.), letter of May 17, 1967.

"Committees (opposed to sonic booms) are being formed—many of them, like the Citizens League Against the Sonic Boom, numbering among their membership distinguished scientists, writers, and conservationists."

DR. WILLIAM H. STEWART, M.D., U.S. Surgeon General and Head of U.S. Public Health Service in keynote address at the June 14, 1968 National Conference on Noise as a Public Health Hazard.

Chapter 1

$64 Billion Question

Introduction

Airplane builders here and abroad are enthralled in a grandiose dream: the dream of building $64,000,000,-000 worth of supersonic transport planes. They dream of revolutionizing long-range travel, improving the respective countries' balance of payments, creating more than 200,000 jobs, gaining prestige, and reaping handsome profits.

But to many people the dream is a nightmare. They dread the sonic booms the supersonic transport planes would produce, and estimate that the sonic booms would startle hundreds of millions of people each day and damage at least a million houses a week. They expect that such planes would be dangerous and almost prohibitively expensive. They believe that widespread use of the planes would hurt, rather than help, the balance of payments, and they are convinced that the project as a whole would be a financial failure and would leave the taxpayers out-of-pocket to the tune of about $5 billion.

Here in the U.S.A. where there is as yet no supersonic transport plane but only a mass of drawings and reports prepared by Boeing Company and associated manufacturers, the issue is a simple one: Should our Government push the Boeing project and support it with billions of dollars? Or should the project be dropped? Most of the facts, pro and con, are easily stated. The final decision should be made—not just by the aviation industry and

1

its partisans in Washington, D.C.—but also by the people who would be providing most of the money: the taxpayers.

President Nixon gave his views in an announcement of September 23, 1969, proclaiming that we must go ahead with the project. How he arrived at this conviction is mysterious, since most of the members of his own *SST ad hoc Review Committee* came to the opposite conclusion (their reasons are set forth in Appendix 4). Many Congressmen, and likewise a large segment of our country's press, expressed unhappiness at finding the taxpayers pressured into providing an additional $662 million for the project in the next five years, and perhaps several *billion* dollars more in subsequent years—even though inflation is growing and funds badly needed in much more urgent projects are being cut.

What Is an SST?

An SST (supersonic transport plane) is a commercial airplane that travels routinely at a speed exceeding the speed at which sound travels in the atmosphere. There are no SSTs in use today, but European and Soviet prototypes have been built and are being flight-tested.

What is the speed of sound in the atmosphere? About 760 miles per hour, in air at 60° F at sea level. At high altitude the temperature is lower and therefore the speed of sound is lower. At 65,000 feet altitude, where the typical temperature is far below zero (−80° F), the speed is 650 mph. The speed depends strongly on the temperature of the air but not on the pressure.

An airplane traveling faster than sound is called *supersonic*. At sea level a plane has to fly faster than 760 mph to qualify as supersonic. At 65,000 feet, where the air is colder, a speed exceeding 650 mph qualifies.

Airplane designers usually specify the speed of an

airplane *relative to the speed of sound under the given conditions* (given altitude and temperature). Speeds of one, two, three times the speed of sound are called Mach 1, Mach 2, Mach 3, after the Austrian physicist Ernst Mach. In −80° F air at 65,000 feet, speeds of Mach 1, Mach 2, Mach 3 correspond to 650, 1300, and 1950 mph. In 60° F air at sea level, Mach 1, 2, 3 correspond to 760, 1520, and 2280 mph. (In outer space there is no air, and consequently no sound. Thus astronauts do not use the Mach designation.)

Special Consequences of Supersonic Speed

To the airplane designer the distinction between subsonic speed and supersonic speed is of great importance. When an SST is propelled through the air at a speed faster than sound travels (faster than Mach 1), the resistance of the air increases enormously. Also, the impact of the air on the front portions of the fuselage and wings heats these portions to several hundred degrees Fahrenheit—as hot as a smoking frying pan. To reduce the resistance or *drag,* the SST designer specifies an extremely long and slender shape of fuselage. The frontal surfaces must be of material capable of withstanding the high temperatures produced by the impacting airstream. Much more powerful engines are needed. Fuel consumption is much greater and an additional fifty to one hundred tons of fuel are required. New problems of stability, rigidity, and maneuverability arise. New and impressive dangers threaten. And—most important to the people down below—a widespread, jolting shockwave, or *sonic boom,* is produced.

When a plane flies along a straight route at supersonic speed, it creates an extremely energetic shockwave. The shockwave has the shape of a cone, something like an ice-cream cone lying on its side. More exactly, the plane creates *two* cone-shaped waves that nest close together; one originates at the nose of the plane and the other at the tail.

The conical shockwaves are discussed at length in Chapter 3. Here we need only recognize that they spread out fast and far, eventually attaining a width of 10 to 80 miles, depending on the weight, shape, and altitude of the plane. They spread downward also, striking the earth and delivering sudden, sledge-hammer-like blows to buildings, people, and everything else encountered.

The area of ground struck by the shockwave from a single supersonic plane is enormous. The width of the affected area (width of sonic-boom carpet, or *bang-zone*) is about 50 miles. The *length* of the bang-zone is the entire length of the supersonic flight, typically 2,000 to 3,000 miles. Thus a single SST on a single supersonic flight from New York to California would bang an area about 50 miles wide by 2,000 miles long, or 100,000 square miles. Typically, such an area—ten times the area of Massachusetts—contains 10,000,000 to 40,000,000 people. One plane, on one flight, could bang more people than there are in all of Canada, and twice as many as there are in the entire continent of Australia! (The Federal Aviation Administration (FAA), although empowered by Congress in HR-3400 of July 1968 to ban SST supersonic flight over U.S. territory, has consistently declined to do so, as indicated in Chapter 6.)

A sonic boom is not a bomb. But booms and bombs have a kinship: both produce energetic shockwaves that strike without warning; both damage houses and frighten people; both are alien to peaceful living in civilized communities. The shockwave from a single SST flight across the U.S.A. or across Europe would bang more people than would be jolted by the explosion of a dozen World-War II blockbuster bombs.

Fallacy of "Breaking the Sound Barrier"

The sonic-boom shockwave travels along behind the supersonic plane throughout the *entire length* of the supersonic flightpath, striking—i.e., banging—virtually everything along the way. Until recently most persons assumed (mistakenly) that the boom occurs only momentarily, that is, only at the instant when the speed of the plane first reaches the speed of sound (Mach 1). And when the speed is *above* Mach 1, there is no longer any sonic boom (they mistakenly assumed). In fact, the boom occurs *all the way along the supersonic flight*. A boom is a steady and continuous result of flight at speed exceeding Mach 1. Thus the damage to buildings and the annoyance to people are not local effects, but extremely widespread effects.

Military Supersonic Planes

Supersonic flight by military planes has been a commonplace for a decade. First-class fighter planes can travel at supersonic speed, and some types of bombing planes likewise.

Most persons in America and Europe have heard sonic booms from military planes and thousands of persons have found their homes to have been damaged by these booms. U.S. homeowners have filed damage claims aggregating more than $30,000,000. The U.S. Air Force has issued a pamphlet, *Sonic Boom Background Information* (U-1),* which contains a frank admission that sonic booms are highly annoying and do real damage to buildings. It has issued flight regulations intended to limit the intensity of booms and limit the locations at which sonic booms may be produced by its planes.

Having only 10 to 20 percent the weight of the proposed Boeing SST, the typical military supersonic plane

---

* These Reference numbers refer to documents listed in the author's appended Bibliography, Page 147ff.

has a much less intense boom—if the flight altitudes are comparable. But if such a plane flies at exceptionally low altitude it produces a boom intense enough to cause a disaster. On several occasions such planes have done $500,000 damage in a few seconds, as discussed in Chapter 4.

The main sonic boom tests made in recent years were carried out with booms from military planes. Usually these planes were flown at altitudes that supposedly enabled them to simulate, at the city beneath, the boom intensity that the SSTs would produce. But in the most extensive tests, the Oklahoma City tests discussed in Chapter 4, the booms were only half as intense as the SST's boom would be.

Three Kinds of SSTs

Three kinds of supersonic transport planes (SSTs) have been designed: an Anglo-French version, a Soviet version, and, in the U.S.A., a Boeing version. See Figure 1.

Anglo-French SST. A combined British-French group has developed the Concorde SST which has a capacity of 110 to 132 passengers, a speed of 1400 mph, and is expected to cost about $21,000,000. If the program is continued and there are no further delays, such planes might be in use in 1973. Two prototypes were built in 1968 and flight tests began in March 1969. Construction of several "pre-production" models is underway.

Soviet SST. The Soviet SST, called the Tu-144, is rather similar to the Concorde. A prototype was built and flight tests began on December 31, 1968.

Boeing SST. The SST contemplated by Boeing Co. and associated manufacturers is the most ambitious of the SSTs, having the largest capacity (298 passengers), highest cruising speed (1800 mph), and greatest estimated cost (about $52,000,000 each). If the program is carried forward and no further delays occur, such planes might be in use by about 1978.

The three kinds of SSTs would, of course, compete

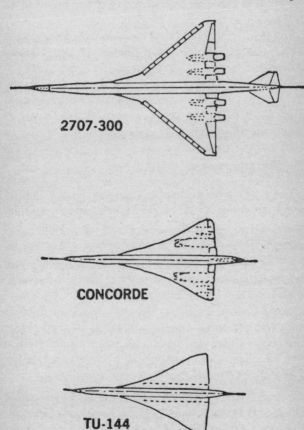

2707-300

CONCORDE

TU-144

Figure 1—The three SSTs: Boeing 2707-300, Anglo-French Concorde, and Soviet Tu-144

with one another. More important, they would find themselves in competition with the *jumbo jet* and *air bus* planes, which are large, low-cost passenger planes that travel just below the speed of sound and so produce no sonic boom at all.

The Jumbo Jet

A jumbo jet is a commercial passenger plane that can carry 350 to 900 passengers over the main transcontinental and transoceanic routes at subsonic speed—about 600 mph, only slightly below the speed of sound.

The most important jumbo jet is the Boeing B-747. Capable of carrying 350 to 490 passengers, this 600 mph plane has a range exceeding 6,000 miles, 50 percent greater than the SST's range. Traveling below the speed of sound and producing no sonic boom, the jumbo jet is permitted to fly over land or water—i.e., anywhere. Being of conventional design (except much bigger) it draws on decades of experience in building safe and efficient planes. Pilots learn to handle it quickly. It fits into existing flight patterns. It provides commodious quarters; seats are wide, there are *two* wide aisles, headroom is generous, and the windows are large. It can take off and land even at moderate-size airports. It has been financed entirely by the aviation industry itself.

Production of this plane is proceeding at a breathtaking pace. Roll-out of the prototype occurred on September 30, 1968, and the first trial flight was on February 10, 1969. By May 1969 a total of 196 orders had been received: 163 for the standard version having a gross weight of 710,000 lb. and 33 for the 747B version weighing 775,000 lb. and designed to carry passengers and freight over distances as great as 6,300 miles. Mass production is underway and the planes will be in widespread use by the end of 1970. Boeing's schedule calls for building one or two of these gigantic planes each week. It expects to sell at least 450 of them by 1976, i.e., *several years* before the Boeing SST would be ready for use.

Airline officials are full of enthusiasm for the B-747 jumbo jet. Mr. H. E. Gray, Chairman of the Board of Pan American Airlines, has said this plane "will obsolete" some of our old aircraft, because it will be so very much cheaper to operate. According to *Interavia* for December 1968, the B-747 will "fly faster and at 30% lower seat-mile cost than even the 707-320B."

Lockheed has designed a jumbo jet having twice the capacity of the Boeing B-747. Its program is still in an early stage, although the Air Force cargo version is already an accomplished fact.

The Air Bus

An air bus is a commercial passenger plane designed to carry about 200 to 300 passengers over medium-length routes (1,500 to 3,000 miles, ordinarily). It is a subsonic plane, produces no sonic boom, and is permitted to fly over land and water. It serves as a shorter-range companion to the jumbo jet. However, one type of air bus is to have a range of 4,500 miles, making it a strong competitor for transoceanic service.

As we shall see in Chapter 10, the jumbo jets and air busses have many advantages over the SST. In fact they have practically *every* advantage except the extra-high speed. (Extra-high speed is of dubious advantage if it entails new kinds of risks, higher fares, and additional causes of delays, discussed in Chapters 7 and 8.)

Chapter 2

SST Design

Aluminum or Titanium?—A Crucial Choice

The most important choice an SST designer can make is the choice of metal to be used in the airplane's exterior. Aluminum and titanium are the two main contenders. The choice strongly influences the design of the plane—and determines the upper limit on cruising speed.

Aluminum (atomic number 13) has low tensile strength and a low melting temperature (660° C). An aluminum plane cannot be permitted to fly faster than about 1400 or 1500 mph because at higher speeds the frontal portions could become so hot as to soften significantly, and dangers from excessive strain, metal fatigue, etc., could arise. The attraction of aluminum is that it is cheap and satisfactory methods of fabricating it are well established.

Titanium (atomic number 22) is exceedingly strong. It has high tensile strength, high softening temperature, and high melting temperature (1800° C). Thus a titanium airplane wing can withstand the severe heating that results when the plane knifes through the air at 1800 mph. Methods of fabricating structures of titanium were almost unknown a few years ago, but much research has been done on this subject in recent years; see, for example, the May 1968 *Aerospace Technology*.

The Anglo-French designers chose aluminum—to save time and money. They could start design and construction almost immediately, using a readily available material and standard fabrication techniques. They accepted the fact that their plane could not be permitted to fly faster than about 1500 mph. The particular aluminum alloy chosen was Hiduminium RR58, which withstands higher temperature than pure aluminum does.

The Soviet designers likewise chose aluminum and accepted the resulting limitation on speed. However, they employed titanium in certain crucial portions of the frontal surfaces.

Boeing engineers, doing their design work some years later, specified titanium in order that their SST would be able to withstand temperatures produced by an 1800 mph airstream. Staggering problems were presented: new sources of titanium metal would be needed and new methods of fabricating it into intricate structures would be required. Long series of tests would be necessary to show what strength and durability had been achieved. Novel problems in corrosion were encountered. But the designers held out for the 1800 mph speed —and titanium. Indeed, strong arguments can be made that if an SST is to be built at all, it should be a very fast one: to accept all the obstacles and costs entailed in supersonic flight merely for a *small* increase in speed would be eminently unwise.

Anglo-French Concorde SST

History. An agreement between the British and French governments to embark on a joint program of designing and building two models of a Concorde SST was signed in November 1962, with the expectation that the cost of the program would be $360,000,000.

By 1967 construction was well underway. The British effort was concentrated at the British Aircraft Corporation (BAC) of Bristol, England. The French effort was managed by Sud-Aviation of Toulouse, France.

The first prototype, called Concorde-001, was assembled at Toulouse. Roll-out was on September 1, 1968. The first (low speed) flight was on March 2, 1969, and the first supersonic flight was on October 1, 1969. The second prototype, Concorde-002, was assembled at Bristol; the first flight was on April 9, 1969. Late in 1969 the construction of several "pre-production" models was well underway.

Design. The Concorde is a highly streamlined mid-wing monoplane with a fixed triangular (delta-shaped) wing and four engines mounted at the rear. The nose is hinged, and droops for improved pilot visibility during landing. Other specifications are:

Length, width, height: 193 ft., 84 ft., 38 ft.

Weight at take-off, fully loaded: 367,000 lb.

Maximum fuel load: 24,000 gallons (almost 100 tons)

Engines: four Bristol-SMECMA Olympus 593 engines of 35,000 lb. thrust each.

Take-off speed: 227 mph (almost twice that of many existing planes).

Take-off distance: 10,900 ft. (more than two miles)

Cruising speed and altitude: Mach 2.0 (about 1400 mph) at 55,000 ft.

Number of passengers: 100 to 132.

Range with full load: 4000 statute miles.

Take-off noise, landing noise: substantially greater than for today's commercial planes. See Chapter 9.

Sonic boom overpressure: about 2.0 pounds per square foot. Bang-zone extends entire length of supersonic flightpath and is about 40 miles wide.

Speed at approach to landing: 180 mph, with 10.8 degree upward tilt.

Technical Difficulties and Alterations

Even before the Concorde's subsonic test-flights were

completed, several shortcomings of the design became apparent. In the spring of 1968 Sir George Edwards, Managing Director of BAC, said that there was concern about rudder flutter problems and excessive temperature in the nacelles during reverse thrust of the engines. Difficulties were encountered also with the plane's droop nose, the highly complex system of fuel transfer for in-flight trim, and the brakes. Early in 1969 Mr. A. W. Benn, British Minister of Technology, announced in Parliament that the two pre-production models of the Concorde were to be modified in many ways, including: changing the shape of leading edges of wing, wing tips, and extreme end of fuselage; increasing the fuel capacity; modifying the engines in several ways. The pre-production models are to be 25 tons heavier and 9 feet longer than the prototypes, according to *Aviation Week* of February 3, 1969; see also the October 1969 Congressional *Hearings,* item U-5 in the bibliography appended to this book.

Schedule. Subsonic testflights of the two prototypes continued throughout 1969. Test flights at supersonic speed started late in 1969 and are to continue in 1970. Routine production of Concordes for commercial use might begin in 1970 or 1971 and if no further difficulties arise the planes could be in commercial use by 1973.

Soviet Tu-144 SST

The Soviet Tu-144 SST, built at the Tupolev plant at Shukovsky near Moscow and named after its designer, Andrei N. Tupolev, has a fixed, swept-back, delta-shaped wing much like that of the Concorde. Here too the principal metal used is an aluminum alloy, with some use of titanium also, and the plane's speed must be limited to about 1500 mph. The windows are 8 inches in diameter.

The plane is smaller than the Concorde and carries

fewer passengers: about 98 to 120, with three hostesses and a crew of three. Maximum loaded weight is 330,000 lb. The plane is powered by four Kuznetsov NK-144 two-shaft turbofan engines mounted in pairs in two nacelles beneath the fuselage centerline. Each engine provides 18,600 lb. thrust during normal operation and 38,500 lb. when the afterburners are in use.

Recent design modifications include greater camber of wingtips and a slight widening of the forward part of the wing in order to improve performance at the lower end of the speed range. Other characteristics are: length 186 feet, wingspan 72 feet, operational ceiling 65,000 feet. The sonic boom overpressure is said to be similar to that of the Concorde.

The first (subsonic) flight was on December 31, 1968, and the first supersonic flight was on June 5, 1969. It is rumored that such planes could be in use in 1972.

Boeing B-2707-300 SST

Early History. The history of the Boeing SST project is one of repeated disappointments. Three separate stages may be discerned, and each was discouraging to the SST proponents.

The first stage (1960-1964) began with the Congressional hearings of May 1960 by the House Committee on Science and Astronautics. Believing that the development of an SST would be reasonably economical and told by the promoters that the sonic boom problem would not be serious, Congress provided, in August 1961, $11,000,000 for the first year of a two-year research program. In January 1963 President John F. Kennedy created a cabinet-level coordinating committee, and the National Aeronautics and Space Administration (NASA) awarded short-term design-study contracts to Boeing and Lockheed. Airframe and systems-study contracts were awarded in April, and on June 3 the President announced his decision to proceed with an SST design and construction program. (He promised that "In no event will the Government investment be permitted to exceed $750 million," according to the *Congressional Record* of October 31, 1969, p. H-10432.)

In July and August of 1963 requests for proposals as to components and system designs were issued. In November Congress voted $60,000,000 for a Fiscal Year 1964 budget for SST design. In January 1964 three airframe manufacturers and three engine manufacturers submitted preliminary design proposals. SST advocates were hopeful that SSTs might be in commercial use by 1968. But in April 1964 President Lyndon B. Johnson announced that none of the designs was satisfactory. Four years had passed, and still no satisfactory design existed.

The second stage (1964-1968) was more dramatically unsuccessful. In May 1964 the President called for contracts for further design proposals, and in June the Government arranged six-month contracts with Boeing and Lockheed (for airframe design) and General Electric and Pratt & Whitney (for engine design). In July 1965 the President announced an 18-month extension of this work and indicated that $140,000,000 would be requested for Fiscal Year 1966. On December 31, 1966, the Government announced its decision in favor of the Boeing swing-wing airframe design and the General Electric engine. ". . . climaxing three-and-one-half years of intense competition" (*Fortune,* February 1967). In 1967 and 1968 the Federal Aviation Administration announced that the Boeing swing-wing design was excellent and that the manufacturer was essentially ready to "start cutting metal." Suddenly, on October 21, 1968, Boeing announced the abandonment of the swing-wing design.

What was the ill-fated B-2707-200 swing-wing design? It featured wings that were mounted on gigantic hinges, or bearings. The wings were to be extended (i.e., swung almost straight out to the sides) for take-off and landing or other low-speed flight in order to provide maximum lift. They were to be swung backward and inward, close to the fuselage, for high-speed flight, to reduce the frontal area, reduce drag, and reduce the intensity of sonic boom. With wings extended for take-off, the width of the plane was 180 feet, wider than a football field. The length was 318 feet, longer than a football field. Loaded with 50,000 gallons (almost 200 tons) of fuel and 330 passengers, the plane had a gross take-off weight of 670,000 lb., or 335 tons. The weight of the empty plane was 350,000 lb. Cruising speed was 1800 mph at 65,000 ft. Range was expected to be 4,000 miles (until more accurate estimates showed the range would be drastically less, and the design was abandoned).

Aviation writers had hailed the swing-wing design as offering "the best of both worlds." With the wings extended, reasonably low take-off speed and landing speed were achieved, they said, and subsonic flight (when and if required, e.g., over heavily populated areas) would be efficient. With the wings swept back, supersonic flight would be highly efficient. The design was called daring and successful, and Boeing's choice of this feature was one of the main reasons why, late in 1966, the Federal Aviation Administration chose this design rather than the conventional, fixed-wing design proposed by Lockheed. No adequate statement has been provided by the FAA as to why the impracticability of the swing-wing design had not been appreciated earlier.

The third stage (1968 to date) was begun in great agony for Boeing Co. As explained in detail in the October 1968 *Fortune,* Boeing engineers had for months sought frantically for a successful design that could be announced before the failure of the swing-wing design became generally known. Some Boeing engineers clung to the hope that the swing-wing design might yet be improved and made acceptable; but Boeing's main effort was on finding an alternative—quickly.

On October 21, 1968, Boeing made its announcement: "The Boeing Company formally announced . . . that it had abandoned its swing-wing design for the U.S. supersonic airliner in favor of a relatively conventional fixed-wing plane" (*New York Times,* October 22, 1968). The new design, called B-2707-300, was submitted to the FAA on January 15, 1969, in not-fully-complete form.

The new design had many hallmarks of failure. It was to have a 40 percent more severe sonic boom than the earlier version (and meanwhile additional sonic boom tests had been completed and showed that the SST's boom, far from being marginally acceptable to people, would be about *twenty times* too intense to be acceptable, as explained in Chapter 6). The passenger capacity of the new design was less, the take-off speed was much greater, and the expected date of first use was put off four years—until 1978. Lacking the glamorous swing-wing, and with a clear resemblance to the Concorde design and to the rejected Lockheed design of 1966, the new design had sharply reduced popular appeal.

Meanwhile the jumbo jet and air bus programs were leaping ahead. Orders had skyrocketed. The room left for SST sales had shrunk alarmingly.

Pro-SST persons had hoped that President Nixon would announce his decision by February 1969. To their chagrin, seven months were to elapse before, on September 23, 1969, he announced his pro-SST decision, a decision that ran counter to the recommendations of most of the members of his *SST ad hoc Review Committee* (see Appendix 4). In subsequent debates in Congress vigorous protests were made by many senators and representatives, and a large segment of the press questioned the logic of building an extra-dangerous, extra-costly boom-spewing airplane at a time when essential health programs were being curtailed because of lack of funds. The go-ahead given to the two prime contractors, Boeing Co. and General Electric Co., was partially overshadowed by the rapidly growing nationwide doubts as to the feasibility, or even the desirability, of the SST project.

New Design. The detailed design of the Boeing B-2707-300 SST has not been published by the FAA, but many of the main design features are now known, for example from the October 1969 *Congressional Hearings* (U-5) and recent issues of technical journals on aeronautics. As indicated in Figure 2, the plane would have a fixed wing, of triangular (delta) shape, swept back at 50°—less sharply than in the Concorde. There is an independent horizontal tail. The four engines, mounted independently beneath the wings, are similar to those planned for the earlier design: four GE-4 afterburning turbojet engines of 60,000 to 67,800 lb. thrust each. Other characteristics of the engines are: 633 lb/sec airflow; 2000° F turbine inlet temperature; 308-inch length; 89½ inch maximum diameter; 11,300 lb. weight (per General Electric Co. brochure AEC-240R-6/68 (10M)).

Other specifications are:

Length, width, and height: 298 ft., 143 ft., 52 ft.

Weight at take-off, fully loaded: 750,000 lb. (375 tons).

Fuel: 50,000 gal. (almost 200 tons) of commercial kerosene.

Take-off speed: 220 mph (much faster than today's commercial planes).

Take-off distance: 10,300 ft. (almost two miles).

Cruising speed and altitude: 1800 MPH (Mach 2.7) at 65,000 ft.

Number of passengers: 298.

Range with full load: 4,000 statute miles.

Take-off noise: expected to be greater than for present-day jets. A major worry. Use of afterburning engines makes extremely high noise levels inevitable. See Chapter 9.

Sonic boom overpressure: 3.5 psf during climb after reaching Mach 1, and 2.1 during cruise, i.e., about 40 percent greater than for the abandoned swing-wing design. See Chapter 6.

Speed on approach to landing: 178 mph (with 10.1° upward tilt).

Technical Difficulties. The story of the technical difficulties encountered in designing the Boeing SST is a long one. The reader is referred to the detailed accounts in *Fortune* (M-2) and in the Ocober 1969 Congressional *Hearings* (U-5). Major problems were encountered in connection with rigidity, stability, weight, range, engine

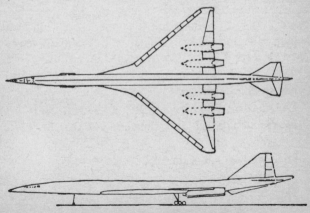

Figure 2—Boeing SST, 2707-300

noise, sonic boom, fuel leak, lightning and fire danger. Many of the problems have not yet been solved.

Schedule. SST proponents say that if all of the pressing problems are solved promptly a first prototype of Boeing SST could be ready for trial flight in 1972, and if no serious difficulty then shows up and adequate (multi-billion-dollar) financing materializes, production planes could be in use by 1978.

Subcontractors. Boeing Co. has general responsibility for the SST other than the engines, which are the responsibility of General Electric Co. The main subcontractors are: Aerojet-General Corp., Aeronca, Inc., Avco Corp., Fairchild Hiller Corp., LTV Aerospace Corp., North American Rockwell Corp., Northrop Corp., Rohr Corp.

Chapter 3

Sonic Boom: What Is It?

The Signature

The sonic boom is a sudden pressure disturbance, or *shockwave*, in air. When an SST flies at great altitude over a house, the pressure near the house remains normal (14.7 lb/sq. in.) at first. But as the shockwave strikes the house, the pressure increases almost instantaneously—in about 0.003 seconds—buffeting the entire house and knocking the upper portion sidewise (by about 0.02 inch typically, for a light, wooden frame house, as indicated in Reference J-1), jarring everything in the house. The pressure wave actually enters the house and is reflected back and forth within each room. Within about 0.02 second the pressure decreases smoothly, and indeed becomes somewhat below normal pressure. Then, again very suddenly, the pressure rises. It rises to the normal pressure, and remains normal thereafter. (Excellent accounts of the physics of sonic booms are to be found in References C-1, U-16, U-18, B-3.)

In summary, the sonic boom is represented by an "N"-shaped pressure-vs.-time graph, such as is shown in Figure 3. Thus two sudden rises in pressure are involved, with an intervening period in which the pressure falls. This curve, or graph, is called the sonic boom *signature*. Planes of different weight, length and shape have slightly different signatures.

21

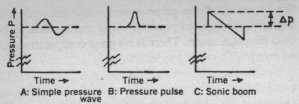

Figure 3—Signatures of simple pressure wave, a pressure pulse, and a sonic boom

Overpressure

The severity of the boom is usually expressed in terms of the sudden rise in pressure, called "$\triangle p$", the *overpressure*. The typical overpressure to be produced at the ground by an SST flying overhead at cruising altitude is about 2.0 to 3.0 pounds per square foot (psf).

Persons writing about sonic booms often refer to the "nominal overpressure." This is simply the calculated value of overpressure that would be expected if there were no atmospheric focusing effects or other modifying effects. The actual overpressure at any one spot may differ considerably from the nominal overpressure for reasons discussed in a later section of this chapter.

The Boeing SST would produce booms of about 3.5 psf during the early part of supersonic flight and 2.1 during cruise, as indicated in Chapter 2. (See also page 264 of the *Hearings* (U-5), where an FAA official compares the boom overpressure of the earlier design and present design thus: "The last figure we had on the variable sweep wing for maximum overpressure during acceleration was around 2.5 pounds per square foot. The maximum overpressure on the current Dash-300 aircraft is just under 4 pounds per square foot.")

Cause of the Boom

A boom is produced because the air in front of the SST simply has not enough time to get out of the way in normal manner. When a *subsonic* plane flies along, the air ahead of the plane moves aside smoothly with negligible changes in pressure—and moves back in behind the plane again. There is no great compression, and no energetic wave is produced.

But for the SST the situation is utterly different. Because the plane is traveling at a speed faster than sound can travel in air (faster than the typical air molecules travel), the air in front of the plane receives no advance "push" as the plane approaches. Each cubic inch of air remains motionless until the very last instant: not until the plane has approached within a half-inch does the air begin to move out of the way. It must then move out of the way in a few *millionths* of a second.

Its motion is extremely energetic. There is extreme local compression and heating, and a highly energetic shockwave spreads out in a cone. The energy in the shockwave from the plane as a whole is enormous; the power radiated outward in this wave amounts to 10,000 to 50,000 horsepower, comparable to the power requirement of an ocean liner such as the Queen Elizabeth II.

The shockwave travels far, jolting everything it strikes. It continually spreads outward until the diameter is about 40 to 60 miles, beyond which the pressure rise is too small to be significant. See Figure 4. One of the

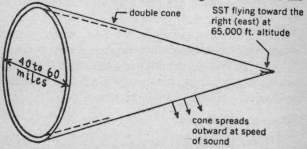

Figure 4—Conical shockwave

two nesting cones is derived from the nose of the plane, and the other from the tail.

Bang-Zone

The bang-zone, or sonic boom carpet, is the portion of the earth's surface struck by the boom from an SST in a single supersonic flight. The bang-zone is as long as the supersonic flightpath itself: if an SST crossing the U. S. flew at supersonic speed for 2,000 miles, the length of the bang-zone would be 2,000 miles. The width of the bang-zone is about 50 miles if the SST is at cruising altitude of 60,000 to 70,000 feet. If the plane flies at lower altitude, the bang-zone is narrower—but the intensity is greater. The width depends also on wind and temperature variations in the atmosphere and may sometimes be as great as 80 miles. The total area of the bang-zone of an SST flying at supersonic speed across the U.S.A. would be about (50) × (2000) or 100,000 square miles—twelve times the area of Massachusetts. A single such flight could boom 10,000,000 to 40,000,-000 people.

A person situated in the bang-zone of a given SST would, of course, be struck by the boom just once—just as a swimmer on a beach is struck just once by the bow wave of a large motorboat cruising parallel to the beach.

Rise Time

The time interval in which the first pressure increase occurs, the *rise time,* is of great importance. Persons who are outdoors find a boom with very short rise time to be far more startling and annoying than one with a long rise time. Even a 0.003-second change in rise time makes a big difference. But persons inside buildings, where reverberation effects play a major role, find booms with larger rise times particularly annoying.

Laboratory-produced, or "simulated," sonic booms often have a rise time much longer than that of an SST's sonic boom, and have relatively little startle effect (U-18, p. 177). Often the overpressures used are far less than those that the SSTs would produce (S-2, U-7). Unfortunately, the investigators reporting the results of simulated sonic booms seldom call attention to the various ways in which the simulated booms are less startling than the SST's booms; see B-5, S-2, U-7.

Impulse and Intensity

Impulse is a term that takes into account not only the pressure rise but also the length of time the pressure acts. Crudely defined, it is the product of *pressure* and *time interval;* more exactly it is the integral of pressure excess with respect to time. The importance of impulse is easily understood: to produce damage, a boom must produce a large pressure and must *sustain* the pressure long enough for it to be effective. Both aspects (pressure and duration) are important. *Impulse* takes both aspects into account.

The SSTs are much longer than typical military supersonic planes and produce pressure pulses (booms) of longer duration. Thus SSTs' booms tend to be more damaging for two reasons: greater overpressure (assuming a given flight altitude) and greater duration of the overpressure. In summary, the impulse is greater. For certain kinds of structures, impulse is the most important quantity and is a better measure of damage-potential than overpressure (L-14, N-6).

The term *intensity* is often used informally to indicate the severity of a sonic boom. When used with greater accuracy, it means a quantity proportional to the square of the overpressure. Thus doubling the overpressure quadruples the intensity.

Superbooms

A superboom is a sonic boom that, at some given location, has an overpressure two or more times the nominal overpressure. (Detailed discussions of superbooms are presented in many reports by Lundberg; see for example Reference L-10. Or see *Aviation Week,* March 27, 1967, or Baxter's impressive monograph, "The SST: From Watts to Harlem in Two Hours," B-3.)

There are four main causes of superbooms:

1. *Transition through Mach 1.* When an airplane is accelerating and reaches a speed very slightly exceeding the speed of sound in the atmosphere, the sonic boom produced is especially intense, and is a superboom. Obviously, such superbooms are produced just locally. The ground area struck by such a superboom is small. The area has a curved, horseshoe shape; the over-all width of the horseshoe is 10 to 25 miles and the length, measured parallel to the flightpath, is only 50 to 300 feet; the total area is about one square mile (L-16).

2. *Atmospheric Focusing.* If there are varying temperatures and wind velocities in the air through which the sonic-boom shockwave travels, focusing effects may occur. Consequently the overpressure at the ground is not uniform but varies considerably from one location to another. Some locations may experience little or no boom while others experience superbooms. A given house may receive twice the overpressure received by a neighbor's house a few hundred feet away. Typically, about one house in 500 in a given bang-zone will be hit by a double-overpressure boom and about one in 10,000 will be hit by a triple-overpressure boom, when an SST flies past at cruising altitude (L-16). Superbooms produced by atmospheric focusing are more frequent in summer than in winter (*Aviation Week,* November 27, 1967).

3. *Reflection Effects.* If a sonic boom strikes smooth

hard ground, or a city street, or a massive building, it is reflected. In the local region of reflection the boom overpressure may be twice the free-field overpressure. Ordinarily, boom overpressure is measured very close to the ground and accordingly the routine doubling that occurs here is already included in the measurement. Reflections from a deeply curved valley floor or from a cluster of massive buildings can sometimes triple the overpressure.

4. *Maneuver of the SST.* If the SST follows a curved path (up and down, or right and left), focusing effects occur and the boom travels with different intensities in different directions. Some houses may escape almost entirely; others may be struck with superbooms. Drastic changes in *speed* of the plane may also produce local superbooms.

Importance of Superbooms. Though relatively rare, superbooms would be of great importance, for several reasons. First, the *absolute number* of buildings that would be struck by superbooms in a single day (if 200 SSTs were flying routinely over populated land at supersonic speed) would amount to about 2,000,000, and the number of man-superbooms per day would be about 10,000,000. Second, doubling the overpressure of a boom may result in damage *more* than twice the damage produced by a normal boom: a structure that remains unscathed by a 3 psf boom may be seriously damaged by a 6 psf boom. Third, because the superbooms are erratic, rather than predictable, engineers cannot plan ahead of time to make the booms of "just barely tolerable" intensity. Fourth, the existence of superbooms means that people must abandon any slight hope they may have had that they would "get used to the booms." Even if a man somehow became accustomed to 2 psf booms, he would be much startled and annoyed by a 4 or 8 psf boom. By way of analogy, a typical person never quite "gets used to" lightning, because there is always the chance that the next lightning stroke will strike his house and paralyze or kill him. Lightning strokes—and superbooms —are too variable to get used to.

It is expected that the Concorde SSTs would produce frequent superbooms with overpressure of 3 to 6 psf and the Boeing SSTs would produce frequent super-booms with 4 to 8 psf.

Chapter 4

Sonic Boom Damage:
Demonstrations and Tests

In the last ten years much has been learned as to the damage sonic booms do to buildings. Many kinds of military planes have been flying routinely at supersonic speed, and on several occasions such planes have been used in carefully planned sonic boom tests over cities or over special testing grounds. There have been several dramatic demonstrations of boom damage potential when pilots accidentally flew too low and created veritable disasters, to the embarrassment of aviation officials.

Disastrous Demonstrations

Ottawa, Canada. Late in 1959, at the Uplands Airport at Ottawa, an F-104 supersonic fighter plane flew at 500 feet altitude above the multi-million-dollar terminal building, producing a sonic boom that broke most of the windows, twisted metal window frames, and jarred loose the insulation cemented to the underside of the roof. The damage was estimated at $500,000 (D-1, H-2; also *Mechanix Illustrated,* October 1965).

Oklahoma City. In the mid-1950's a military plane flew low over the Will Rogers Terminal at the Oklahoma City Airport and delivered a sonic boom that caused $500,000 damage (*Congressional Record,* June 10, 1968, p. H-4756; also H-2).

Colorado Springs. On May 31, 1968, an F-105 plane flew at supersonic speed 500 feet above the Air Force

Academy at Colorado Springs, Colorado. The sonic boom broke $50,000 worth of windows and showered broken glass onto persons attending graduation ceremonies. Fifteen persons were injured (*New York Times,* June 1, 1968, front page article with photograph of damage).

White Sands, New Mexico. In January 1965 at the White Sands Missile Range, New Mexico,

> "Gordon Bains, director of the nation's SST program, was telling newsmen that many persons who claimed their property had been damaged by sonic booms were only imagining the damage. 'I believe there's a great deal of psychology in this,' he explained, when ——WHAM! A jet fighter pilot in an F-104 broke through the sound barrier at an altitude of only 500 feet. The booming shockwave which followed blew out two 7 by 12 feet plate-glass windows . . ." (*Parade,* January 17, 1965).

The 40 psf sonic boom ". . . knocked out a store front and windows all over town. It also dislodged a ten-pound window screen that hit an FAA official on the head . . . no one knows yet how much damage was done" (*Mechanix Illustrated,* October 1965).

Palmdale, California. A minor disaster at Palmdale, California, was described thus: in *Air Travel* for June 1967:

> "The only sonic boom I ever experienced close at hand scared the bejeezus out of me and a number of other newsmen who had been flown by North American Aviation to Palmdale (near Los Angeles) for the flight demonstration of a new supersonic fighter aircraft. The pilot, eager to give the assembled reporters and photographers a reasonably close view of the plane, made a supersonic pass over the field at a little too low altitude and shattered most of the plate glass windows and doors of the airport terminal building."

Kelowna, British Columbia. On August 6, 1969, a U.S. Navy F4 acrobatic plane accidentally exceeded the speed of sound while flying at 300 feet altitude above Kelowna, B.C., with the result that "about 75 percent of the windows in an eight-block area of downtown Kelowna were reduced to shards. Damage was estimated at $250,000. Seven persons were cut by flying glass. Heavy plate-glass windows splintered and pieces flew into the streets. Glass went all over the place" (Toronto *Globe and Mail,* August 8, 1969).

These disasters were caused by sonic booms having 10 to 20 times the overpressure that SSTs would produce when flying at prescribed altitude. They have nothing to do with the SST problem—except in the unlikely event that an SST pilot, in some emergency, fli s his plane at supersonic speed at lower-than-permissible altitude over a city. Such a flight could do $10 million or more damage to houses, factories, or churches, and flying glass could injure hundreds of persons.

Let us now consider the effects of sonic booms comparable to those which the SSTs would produce routinely.

Sonic-Boom Tests over U.S. Cities

As soon as it was realized that extra-severe sonic booms could do serious damage to buildings, the U.S. Government, hoping to go forward with its SST program, planned several series of sonic boom tests over cities. Aviation officials expected to demonstrate that *typical* booms do not damage buildings and do not annoy people appreciably. No SSTs existed. Therefore the tests were carried out with military supersonic planes. Being smaller and lighter than SSTs, the military planes normally produced booms far milder than SSTs would produce. To compensate for this—partially, at least— the pilots flew their military planes at somewhat lower altitude. (As it turned out, the overpressures employed in the Oklahoma City tests were only about half those predicted for the Boeing SST.) Being shorter than SSTs, the military planes' booms had a shorter duration and smaller impulse.

The Government has published detailed reports on these tests, and it is a simple matter to compile statistics on the actual damage payments made (i.e., payments made up until the time the reports were written; many damage claims were then still in litigation). Additional information is now available from statements by the U.S. Department of Justice and from Federal Court decisions.

St. Louis, 1961–1962. There were 150 supersonic flights made over St. Louis, Missouri, in 1961 and 1962. The population of St. Louis was then about 750,000. Thus the total number of man-booms was (150) × (750,000) or about 113,000,000. (A man-boom is an individual act in which one boom strikes one person.) The official reports indicate that about 5,000 persons complained, 1,624 filed damage claims, and 825 of the claims were paid (U-14). The total payment was $58,684, corresponding to $519 per million man-booms (C-5, C-6).

Oklahoma City, 1964. This is the most extensive sonic boom test ever made. For five months, sonic booms were inflicted on Oklahoma City every hour on the hour (daytime only). Boom overpressure was monitored and the flights were arranged to produce gradually increasing overpressure from month to month; the average overpressure was about 1.3 pounds per square foot (psf). The 1,254 flights over this city of 324,000 inhabitants produced 406,000,000 man-booms; 15,452 persons complained and 4,901 persons filed damage claims (U-8, U-10, Z-1). The largest payment was $10,000 to Mr.

Bailey Smith of 1803 NE 67 St., for serious damage done
to his almost-new $90,000 house (D-1; also personal
communication from Mr. Smith). Many of the largest
claims were in litigation for many years. As a consequence of a 1968 verdict by the U.S. Tenth District
Court and a verdict of March 1969 by the U.S. Tenth
Circuit Court upholding that original verdict, a total of
$94,015 damage payments was awarded in 1969 to
supplement payments of $19,355 on claims settled in
previous years. The aggregate payment was $123,070.
This corresponds to $303 per million man-booms (C-5,
C-6). (In November 1969 $128,788 in additional
claims was still pending and is expected—following recent precedent—to be settled in favor of the homeowners concerned; see letter of November 21, 1969,
by A. C. Latina of the U.S. Department of Justice.)

Oklahoma City residents found that sonic booms
broke window panes, cracked walls of plaster, tile, and
bricks. They found that the booms jiggled shelves and
caused dishes, tumblers, and vases to "jiggle" and eventually fall to the floor and break.

Chicago, 1965. The 49 flights over the city's 3,550,000
inhabitants resulted in 174,000,000 man-booms, 7,128
complaints, 3,156 damage claims, and 1,464 payments
aggregating $116,229, corresponding to $668 per million man-booms (U-15, A-3 p. 270).

Milwaukee, 1965. The 61 flights over 741,000 inhabitants resulted in 45,000,000 man-booms, 953 complaints, 639 damage claims, and 259 claim payments
aggregating $12,652, corresponding to $281 per million
man-booms (A-3).

Pittsburgh, 1965. The 50 flights over 604,000 inhabitants resulted in 30,000,000 man-booms, 1,848 complaints, 1,102 damage claims, and 503 payments ag-

gregating $30,808, corresponding to $1,027 per million man-booms (A-3).

Edwards Air Force Base, California, 1966–1967. The 367 flights over 45,000 inhabitants resulted in 1,650,000 man-booms, 62 complaints, 19 damage claims, and 16 claim payments aggregating $1,399, corresponding to $848 per million man-booms (B-8). In these tests much attention was given to breakage of window panes both at the Air Force Base itself and in an adjacent village. The investigators went to the trouble of examining the Air Force Base window panes of principal interest *before and after* the booms struck. They found the breakage rate to be 0.127 panes per million pane-booms. (The serious implications of this are discussed in Chapter 6.) The damage found in the nearby village (where verification was made with somewhat less care) was found to be 0.5 panes per million pane-booms, i.e., four times as great (J-1).

Summary of U.S. Test Results

The following table summarizes the results of the main sonic boom tests on buildings. It appears that the typical rate of damage payments was $400 to $700 per million man-booms. A commonly used figure is $600 per million man-booms (C-5, C-6, and *Congressional Record,* June 10, 1968, pp. H-4761-4762). For an estimate of the over-all daily damage that would be done by a fleet of SSTs, see Chapter 6.

Other Experience

U.S. Air Force Experience. U.S. Air Force planes' booms do much damage each year—in routine training flights and exercises. In the three-month period July—September 1967, $3,800,000 in sonic-boom damage claims were presented to the Air Force, according to a statement of February 1, 1968, by Col. W. R. Arnold of the Office of the Judge Advocate General. In Illinois alone more than 1,000 complaints were made in that same period. (*Chicago Tribune,* September 16, 1967).

On August 11, 1966, a boom from an Air Force plane struck the Canyon de Chelly National Monument in Arizona and loosened an estimated 80 tons of rock, which fell on ancient Indian cliff-dwellings and caused them irreparable damage. Additional damage was done by 83 sonic booms in the subsequent four months (*National Parks Magazine,* March 1968; also *American Forests,* March 1967).

On February 21, 1968, booms produced in Mesa Verde National Park by jets from the Strategic Air Command caused 66,000 tons of rock to fall, according to estimates made by Meredith Guillet, Park Superintendent. He found that many of the ". . . several hundred Indian caves in the area have been cracked or damaged by the supersonic flights." The rockslide temporarily closed one of the tourist roads (*Rocky Mt. News,* April 25, 1968; also letter of April 25, 1969, by K. L. Lundquist, Archaeologist, National Park Service, Mesa Verde National Park).

Sonic booms broke three of the glass flowers of the world-famous collection at Harvard University, according to a letter of October 15, 1968, by R. E. Schultes, Curator.

Experience in Europe. The British Government carried out a brief series of sonic boom tests over Bristol and London in the summer of 1967. There were eleven flights, and the sonic-boom overpressures were about half those expected of SSTs. A total of 515 damage payments, totalling $9,981, were made (*Aviation Daily,* January 16, 1969).

In France, booms from military planes damaged the Chateau de Landal at Broualan Village, collapsing a tower, knocking out windows, and damaging a floor

Analysis of Damage Payments from U.S. Sonic Boom Tests

City	Population	Total number of man-booms	Complaints	Claims filed	Claims paid	Amount paid	Amount paid per million man-booms
Oklahoma City (1964)	324,253	406,000,000	15,452	4,901	289	$123,061	$ 303
Chicago (1965)	3,550,404	174,000,000	7,128	3,156	1,464	116,229	668
St. Louis (1961–62)	750,026	113,000,000	5,000	1,624	825	58,648	519
St. Louis (1965)	750,026	17,000,000	1,390	491	215	17,036	1002
Milwaukee (1965)	741,324	45,000,000	953	639	259	12,652	281
Pittsburgh (1965)	604,332	30,000,000	1,848	1,102	503	30,808	1027
Edwards AFB (1966–67)	45,000	1,650,000	62	19	16	1,399	848

Sources: For Oklahoma City: C-6, U-10, U-19, Z-1. For other cities: A-3, B-8, U-14, U-15.

and ceiling. On December 2, 1967, a court in Rennes ordered the French Government to pay $11,550 in damages (*Philadelphia Enquirer,* December 3, 1967). Other booms from military planes have damaged historic buildings in France, as indicated in an illustrated article in *Les Monuments Historiques de la France* (P-2). On August 2, 1967, at Mauran, a sonic boom caused partial collapse of a barn, killing three persons (*New York Times,* August 3, 1967).

In southwest Germany, sonic booms from jet fighters necessitated the closing of the 18th century abbey church at Neresheim, near Aalen. The sonic booms seriously damaged timbers in the roof, which is now in danger of collapse (*London Times,* June 19, 1967).

In Switzerland sonic booms have triggered avalanches.

Types of Damage

In general, sonic booms from SSTs have done many kinds of damage. They have:

Cracked and shattered glass windows.

Cracked plaster walls and dislodged loose plaster.

Cracked masonry.

Cracked highly strained foundations of buildings that were poorly constructed or were situated on ground that had undergone settlement.

Cracked various kinds of brittle objets d'art and fragile antiques.

Jiggled and vibrated shelves, causing dishes, tumblers, and vases to jiggle sidewise and fall onto the floor and break.

Set off burglar alarms.

Triggered rock slides and avalanches.

Can a boom really do such damage? How, for example, does it damage plaster? Partial answer is given by measurements made on special test houses subjected to sonic booms at the White Sands Proving Grounds in New Mexico. Delicate strain gauges installed in several of the houses showed that a typical boom of about 2 psf overpressure jolts a typical small dwelling so violently that the building as a whole is momentarily distorted (sheared) by about 0.03 inch (N-5). Distorting a plaster wall can crack it, because plaster is extremely brittle. Failure of plaster is somewhat unpredictable; a plaster wall that has withstood 1,000 bombs may crack by the 1,001st boom.

Sonic-boom apologists insist that sonic booms of less than 5 psf overpressure "should not" damage windows or plaster. They say that windows and plaster "will not" crack if they were installed properly and have been maintained properly. But building contractors are notorious for working fast and furiously, and one can hardly expect them to analyze each window pane or plaster wall for built-in strain, or to replace glass or plaster that might perhaps be unusually prone to break. Millions of houses are ten to fifty years old, and inspecting them thoroughly and replacing strained or brittle windows and walls would be fantastically expensive (although this has been seriously proposed; see a recent report by G. M. Lilley, O-1).

Can a sonic boom really trigger a rock slide? It can—it has. It has been found that sonic booms produce seismic waves in the outer portion of the earth's crust—waves sometimes comparable to those produced ". . . by a large pile driver about 200 feet away" (*Journal of the Acoustical Society of America* October 1968; *Science News 94*, November 23, 1968).

Chapter 5

Sonic Boom Annoyance

Kinds of Annoyance

One reason people find the sonic boom annoying is because it is very loud—a sudden loud "bang!" (or sometimes a double bang). Loud noises are distracting and may drown out conversation or music. People dislike loud noises, ordinarily—but may accept very loud music, fire crackers, or such, on appropriate occasions.

The main reason people hate sonic booms is because of *startle effect*. It has been known for decades that a very sudden, loud, *unexpected* noise produces a set of symptoms, or behaviors, called the startle syndrome (B-7). Typically, the syndrome includes hunching the shoulders, pulling the head forward and downward, crouching slightly, releasing adrenaline and increasing the rate of heartbeat. In addition the person may blink, jump, or cry out. Various stomach symptoms may result also, and there may be accompanying feelings of fear, surprise, terror.

The sonic boom is particularly harassing because it has hallmarks of disasters: it is reminiscent of a violent collision of two cars, the detonation of a bomb, or an explosion in a chemical plant a mile or two away. Reacting to a sonic boom with startle, fear, and dread is not merely instinctive but, to some degree, logical and desirable. In these precarious times citizens *should* be wary of sudden noises suggestive of threat to life.

Startle effect may result whether the noise is very

loud or rather gentle, provided it is sudden and unexpected. A person reading a detective story late at night may be badly startled by the noise of an ash-tray falling to the floor. A grandmother may be startled when a small child steals up behind her and says "Boo!" No wonder that the sonic boom—violent enough to shake the entire house and break windows—is startling.

Degree of Annoyance

No adequate definition of degree of annoyance from sonic boom exists. Most acoustics experts, noticing that the booms are loud, have concentrated their efforts on measuring the *loudness* of the boom; they have compared this loudness with the loudness of noises that are more familiar to us—such as airplane take-off noise. To date, no one has developed a business-like method of measuring annoyance due to the startle effect itself.

In the Oklahoma City sonic boom tests, much effort was given to questioning the inhabitants and finding how annoying they considered the booms. Results of the questionnaires show that a majority of the inhabitants found the booms annoying, and, after several months of being boomed every hour during the daytime, 27 percent of the persons interrogated declared that they could never learn to live with such booms (U-10). It is noteworthy that those booms had an average overpressure of about 1.3 psf, i.e., only about half the overpressure that the Boeing SST's booms would have. Also, the booms occurred only during the daytime. They occurred on a fixed schedule and as a consequence some of the surprise element was absent.

In the Edwards Air Force Base tests, reported in detail in the official report N-5, great effort was made to evaluate the annoyance of the booms. Of the 300 persons serving as "test subjects," many were newcomers to sonic booms and many others had been familiar with booms for a year or more. The 300 persons were repeatedly struck by sonic booms from military B-58 supersonic planes, and their opinions were then polled. It was found that 40 per cent of the newcomers and 27 percent of the habituated persons ". . . rated the B-58 booms of nominal peak overpressure 1.69 psf as being less than *just acceptable* to *unacceptable."*

The annoyance would have been much greater if the tests had not been biased in several ways. The people subjected to the booms were warned one or two minutes before each boom, with the result that most of the surprise was eliminated. (If you are sincerely trying to see how startling a sudden loud noise is to a person, you do not tell him just ahead of time, "Get ready! I'm now going to startle you!") The people were adults. They were in good health. They participated in the tests voluntarily. They were relaxed and at leisure when the booms struck. They were in Government-owned houses, and any damage done would be at Government expense. The booms occurred in the daytime only. The boom overpressure (1.69 psf) was much less than the overpressure that the Boeing SSTs would produce (2.0 to 3.5 psf).

The fact that the people objected so strongly to these booms despite these "softening" circumstances is impressive.

Polls taken after the tests in St. Louis and Chicago showed that about 40 percent of the people were greatly annoyed by the booms. In a poll taken in France, 35 percent of the persons questioned said they ". . . definitely could not tolerate" ten booms a day (B-9).

Vulnerable Persons

People differ greatly in their vulnerability to startle. At the one extreme, healthy well-adjusted adults busily engaged in pleasant occupations may experience little annoyance at a sudden loud sound. Such persons may enjoy the sound of gun-fire or a loud clap of thunder. At the other extreme are elderly persons with critical heart conditions, such that even a moderately intense "bang!" may produce spasms, acute pain, and possibly even heart failure. Other vulnerable groups include:

Infants and very old people.

Persons suffering from ulcers and insomnia.

Persons who are very unhappy, irritated, worried, or afraid.

Persons who regard the sudden loud noise as a personal affront—a betrayal of the common man in favor of big business.

Persons with various kinds of mental diseases.

Women in labor, persons in great pain, persons deadly ill.

It is ironic that pro-SST persons who call for extensive sonic boom tests to evaluate the annoyance *never propose carrying out the tests on the most vulnerable groups*. It would be hard to find anyone so callous as to propose booming highly vulnerable people hour after hour, day and night. (Is it not obvious that the booms would inflict great misery on such persons?) Of what value is it to find that some healthy adults can tolerate booms if the vulnerable groups obviously *cannot* tolerate them?

Special Circumstances

Even ordinary adults may be greatly annoyed by sonic booms under special circumstances. Consider, for example:

A musician conducting an orchestra, or an electronic technician making a tape-recording of the music.

A teacher trying to hold the attention of a class.

A clergyman delivering a sermon or conducting a funeral.

A surgeon performing a delicate operation on a patient's eye.

A horse-trainer trying to calm a skittish horse, or a horseback rider following a dangerous mountain trail.

A painter high up on a ladder.

A fireman rescuing an invalid from a brick building, the walls of which might fall at any time.

To any of these persons, a sudden sonic boom may be devastating. A boom can ruin a concert or a tape recording, distract an audience or congregation, cause a surgeon's arm to jerk (and injure the patient), make a horse bolt (and throw the rider), make a man on a ladder lose his balance and fall, cause weakened walls to collapse.

No SST proponent has proposed making sonic boom tests on persons in these special circumstances!

Are people protected from the sonic boom when indoors? In general, no. Tests have shown (B-5, N-5) that persons inside *small* rooms such as bathrooms, kitchens, bedrooms may find the boom *more annoying* than when outdoors. Although the walls of the house reduce the amount of sonic energy entering the house, the shockwave entering a small room is reflected back and forth from wall to wall; thus there is an intensifying effect and also a prolonging effect. And in a city the noise of traffic is less indoors so that the sonic boom may sound especially loud and startling there. Also, indoors there is some danger of being struck by flying glass from a window; parents may fear that their children will be injured.

Are sonic booms more annoying in the country or in the city? This question has never been answered. City dwellers are somewhat accustomed to loud noise, but they may already be exasperated by noise in general and may regard the sonic boom as the last straw. Rural areas tend to be quiet, and a sonic boom there breaks the silence dramatically. One of the main assets of rural areas is the peace and quiet that prevails; rural inhabitants may be resentful at losing this special asset.

Chapter 6

Predicted Sonic Boom Effects
of a Fleet of SSTs

Will Supersonic Flight Over Land Be Banned?

Almost as controversial as the SST project itself is the question: "Will SST supersonic flight over land be banned?" Pro-SST officials are torn between saying Yes and No. They try to calm devotees of peace and quiet by saying, "We realize the sonic boom is very severe and you can rely on us to see that supersonic flight over land is forbidden"—while trying to appeal to the commercial instincts of SST purchasers by saying, "The sonic boom really isn't so bad; people will get used to it; in fact, they will *have* to get used to it; you can't stop progress, and the SSTs *will* be permitted to fly over sparsely populated land and, eventually, perhaps all land."

The double-talk reached its zenith in the Congressional Hearings of October 9, 1969, (U-5, p. 37), when Congressman S. R. Yates tried to get a single unambiguous answer from J. M. Beggs, Undersecretary of Transportation, and J. H. Shaffer, Administrator of the Federal Aviation Administration. He heard Mr. Shaffer testify that "flights at supersonic speed over the United States will not be permitted as long as the sonic boom is an unacceptable factor." The dialogue continued thus:

MR. YATES. What do you mean when you say "as long as the sonic boom is an unacceptable factor?" In the ad hoc committee's report it clearly insisted that somebody ought to say positively that there will be no flights over the United States or over populated areas as long as there is a sonic boom. You do not say that. What you do say is that you will not fly over populated areas as long as it is an unacceptable factor. That is not good enough. FAA wants to fly this plane and I am convinced FAA's decision may be influenced by that fact. FAA is determined to fly this plane. FAA will try to fly this plane whether or not there is a sonic boom, won't it?

MR. SHAFFER. No, sir. I think the language is clear. We say we will not fly supersonically over the United States as long as the sonic boom is unacceptable.

MR. YATES. What does that phrase mean? Do you not mean you hope the people will accept the boom?

MR. SHAFFER. This does not imply that the boom will ever be acceptable. We say as long as it is unacceptable, it will not fly supersonically over inhabited land areas and that is a firm policy statement.

MR. YATES. What is so firm about it? What do you mean by unacceptable? Why can you not say as long as there is a sonic boom it will not be flown over populated areas. Some people say the sonic boom is acceptable. Do you mean unacceptable to you or the average member of the public?

MR. SHAFFER. Unacceptable to the public. As I say, I am not suggesting that it will be acceptable. I am simply saying that as long as it is unacceptable, it will not fly supersonically over the United States.

MR. YATES. You have read this ad hoc committee report?

MR. SHAFFER. Yes, sir.

MR. YATES. You know there are statements in there that there ought to be a unequivocal statement of policy made there will be no flights over land as long as there is a sonic boom, not as long as the sonic boom is unacceptable.

MR. SHAFFER. The President has——

MR. YATES (continuing). Used your phrase.

MR. SHAFFER. No, sir. The President said "will not fly supersonically over land."

MR. YATES. I have not seen that statement by the

President that "It will not fly supersonically over land."

MR. BEGGS. No, he said over populated areas.

MR. YATES. You are not saying that now, are you?

MR. BEGGS. Yes.

MR. SHAFFER. Yes, I am saying it.

MR. YATES. Do I understand you correctly to say now that you will not fly supersonically over populated areas?

MR. SHAFFER. I am saying flights at supersonic speed over the United States will not be permitted as long as the sonic boom is an unacceptable factor.

Mr. YATES. I insist that is not the same thing. You are saying one thing, Mr. Beggs; you are saying you will not fly supersonically over the United States. Mr. Shaffer is saying as long as the boom is unacceptable.

Mr. BEGGS. No, I said we will not fly supersonically over populated areas.

Mr. YATES. Now if you fly supersonically over populated areas, you will get a sonic boom, won't you?

MR. SHAFFER. No, sir.

MR. BEGGS. No, sir, you won't.

MR. YATES. I thought the sonic boom was an inherent characteristic of supersonic flight.

MR. BEGGS. We can get into this later if you like, we have data to support it. You can fly up to Mach 1.15 without laying down a boom on the earth. That is another issue perhaps you may want to explore.

MR. YATES. We will explore it later. This is a most important point as far as I am concerned. I want to make it very clear that I am opposed to flights over land that will produce a sonic boom.

MR. BEGGS. So are we over populated areas.

We quite agree.

MR. MINSHALL. If you will yield, on the morning that this program was announced, at the White House, I remember distinctly Secretary Volpe saying in response to an inquiry from the newsman, that the SST will not fly over populated areas.

MR. BOLAND. Let me read what he said. This is Secretary Volpe, commenting on the President's announcement on the SST:

May I just say one additional thing in regard to the comments of the President. He has told me and he wants the American public to know that this supersonic transport will not be allowed to fly over populated areas unless and until the noise factor comes within acceptable limits.

That is about what Mr. Shaffer said.

Mr. Yates. The point I am making is what may be acceptable limits for the FAA may not be acceptable limits for a person who lives under the flight path. Dr. DuBridge in his ad hoc report says:

The sonic boom is quite unsolved and at best will cause enormous public concern. Surely we must have a policy statement that there shall be no supersonic operations by the SST over any populated areas.

Why is not Dr. DuBridge right?

Are you telling us now there will be no supersonic operations over any populated areas?

Mr. Shaffer. That is correct.

Mr. Beggs. At this time that is exactly right.

Mr. Yates. What do you mean by "at this time?" There you go qualifying it again.

Mr. Shaffer. I do not think so.

Mr. Beggs. I hardly ever say forever on anything.

Mr. Yates. That is what concerns me.

Mr. Beggs. Because I do not know what kinds of developments might be made in terms of lessening the effect of a sonic boom on the earth. There are programs underway right now at the Langley Research Center of NASA investigating configurations of aircraft that will put down no appreciable boom footprint on the earth. You can design toward this objective. I think some day we will learn how to spread this pressure over such a wide area that there will be very little boom effect or overpressure on the earth.

Mr. Yates. The point I am making is that General Maxwell in testimony before this committee said that at Edwards Air Force Base the Air Force officers walk around with the sonic boom bouncing around them without paying any attention to it. And I got the impression from him that in time the average American citizen will be walking around the same way with the sonic boom around him and he will not pay attention to it. I don't accept that. I don't want that citizen to have to live with the sonic boom.

MR. BEGGS. I am in complete agreement with your thought.

MR. YATES. Then, we are in complete agreement that as long as there is a sonic boom from a plane, it will not fly over land.

MR. SHAFFER. Yes, sir. I think the statement said it, too, for the record.

MR. YATES. No; it did not.

The writer believes that FAA officials and other SST advocates still cherish the hope that over land supersonic flights will somehow prove feasible, i.e., that the public can be forced to put up with sonic booms. And he expects that the FAA will continue to leave the door open for SST supersonic flights over populated regions— until overruled by the Congress.

Congressional Efforts to Ban Supersonic Flight Over Land

Several Congressmen, despairing of persuading the FAA to impose a *clear-cut* ban on SST supersonic flight over land, have introduced bills that would "go over the heads" of the FAA and ban such flights. But to date no such bill has succeeded. In 1968 Senator C. P. Case introduced a bill (S.3399) that would have banned SST supersonic flight over U.S. territory; but the bill was not passed. That same year Congressmen T. R. Kupferman, R. L. Ottinger, and ten colleagues introduced a resolution (H. J. Res. 1321 "National Conservation Bill of Rights") that would have banned harassing booms. On February 7, 1969, Senator Case re-introduced his anti-boom bill, but again without success. On September 12, 1969, Congressman A. K. Lowenstein introduced a nearly equivalent bill, without success.

In bill HR-3400, which became law when signed by

President L. B. Johnson on July 24, 1968, the Congress authorized the FAA to set limits on general airplane noise and, incidentally, on SSTs' sonic booms. But Senator Case likened this to "setting the fox to guard the chickens." To date the FAA has declined to set any limit on sonic booms.

Meanwhile a number of cities have attempted to impose local bans. The City Council of Santa Barbara, California, announced a sonic boom ban on September 26, 1967, and, on November 16th of that year Dearborn, Michigan, followed suit. On May 11, 1968, the Welfare Committee of the New York City Council *reported out* favorably a resolution to request the FAA to ban SST landings and take-offs within 100 miles of New York City. Aviation officials regard all such local bans as invalid and without legal force.

Damage Estimates

Suppose the SST proponents' dreams come true: supersonic flight over land is permitted, the people of the world are prosperous and are willing to pay extra-high fares to travel by SST, and large numbers of SSTs are built and put into use. Specifically, suppose the U.S.S.R. sells 200 of its Tu-144 SSTs, the British and French sell 400 Concordes, and Boeing Co. sells 1,200 of its B-2707-300 SSTs (making about $64 billion worth of SSTs in all). How much damage would these planes' booms do to buildings?

No exact answer can be given, but a rough estimate can be made using the damage-payment figures listed in Chapter 4. Suppose each of the 1,800 SSTs makes many trips a day, traveling 9,000 miles a day at supersonic speed. This makes a total of $(1800) \times (9000) = 16,200,000$ SST-supersonic miles a day. Let us assume that half of these miles—8,100,000—are over land. If the bang-zone width is 50 miles, the total number of square-mile-booms will be (8,100,000)x(50) or about 400,000,000.

How much damage would these booms do to buildings? First, let us convert the square-mile-booms to man-booms. Then we can use the actual-damage-payments figure of $600 per million man-booms, based on the major sonic boom tests discussed in Chapter 4. If on the average there are 100 persons per square mile (which may be typical of much of the U.S.A. in 1990), the total number of man-booms per day will be (400,-000,000)x(100) = 40,000,000,000. At $600 per million, this amounts to (40,000)x($600) = $24,000,000 damage per day.

Think of it! A global damage of $24,000,000 per day! To the best of the writer's knowledge, pro-SST persons have never published an estimate of the world-wide daily damage to buildings. Instead, they state repeatedly that a typical boom *should* not damage a *well-made* building. But actual sonic boom tests conducted at enormous expense in Oklahoma City and elsewhere have shown that each million man-booms leads to about $600 damage to houses. The $24,000,000-per-day damage figure is a result of applying simple arithmetic to this figure.

The figure is certainly only an approximate one. In different countries, houses are constructed differently. They may be more vulnerable—or less vulnerable—than houses in Oklahoma City or Chicago. Costs of repair, too, may differ in different countries. But if the figure is wrong, it may well be wrong by being *too low*—because the main sonic boom tests mentioned were conducted with average overpressures of about 1.3 to 1.7 psf whereas the SSTs are expected to produce booms of 2.0 to 3.5 psf overpressure.

Pro-SST persons have claimed that, after a while, most of the easily damaged window panes and plaster walls will have been broken and thereafter the damage rate will decrease. But others point out that this may not be true, for two reasons: (1) The boom overpressure is highly variable, so that a window pane that has withstood hundreds of 2.0 to 3.5 psf booms may nevertheless break when eventually hit by a 6 psf superboom. (2) There may be a cumulative effect such that an initially sturdy plaster wall will gradually deteriorate under repeated sonic booming and eventually will crack.

What does $24,000,000 worth of damage imply physically? At $120 per cracked plaster wall—(a very rough guess)—and $12 per broken window, it could imply, for example, 50,000 ruined plaster walls and 500,000 broken window panes—with $12,000,000 left over to cover damage to ceilings, masonry, dishes, and the like.

Such a figure for window-pane breakage is reinforced (within an order of magnitude) by the special study of window-pane breakage at the Edwards Air Force Base tests (Chapter 4), where the carefully-confirmed breakage rate was found to be 0.127 panes per million pane-booms. Multiplying this by our global estimate of 40,000,000,000 man-booms per day and assuming that typical houses have about 10 panes per occupant, we find that about $(40,000) \times (100) \times (0.127)$ or about 50,000 panes would be broken each day. If, instead, we use the 0.5 panes-per-million-pane-booms figure applicable to the village adjacent to Edwards, we arrive at a figure of about 200,000 broken panes per day.

Think of the work involved in filling out perhaps 500,000 damage claims per day! Think also of the efforts of the people who must process the claims. The number of jobs created in the building of the SSTs might be surpassed by the number of jobs created in processing the claims and repairing the broken windows and cracked walls.

Could the SSTs detour around population centers,

so as to minimize the number of houses boomed? To a very slight extent only. The only merit of the SST is in shortening flight time, and every detour lengthens the route, increases the flight time, and increases the fuel cost. In any event, the maneuverability of the SST is poor. The difficulty and expense of turning a corner were emphasized in a speech of November 15, 1967, by General J. C. Maxwell, then FAA Head of SST Development, at the National Air Safety Meeting: "At supersonic speed we aren't going to be able to afford much turning—it will just use up too much fuel." For an SST to make a sharp turn would take up to 100 miles, so only very slight turns would be feasible. As the SST's bang-zone is 50 miles wide, there would seldom be any chance of avoiding all cities and towns.

Figure 5 shows a typical estimated set of bang-zones over the U.S.A. Obviously the great majority of cities and towns would be included in at least one bang-zone. A typical town would be struck by about 10 to 50 sonic booms per day.

Other bang-zone maps are to be found in a report by the Institute for Defense Analyses, Inc. (I-2) and in various reports by Lundberg; see bibliography. See also *Space Aeronautics,* July 1967, and—for routes near England—*Aviation Week* for October 28, 1968.

Would Metropolitan Areas Be Boom-Free?

An SST produces no sonic boom when first starting up or when completing deceleration prior to landing, because its speed is then subsonic. It produces no boom during about the first 100 miles of its trip and the last 100 miles. Thus a given city will not be boomed by planes taking off from, or landing at, the airport serving that city.

Nevertheless such a city probably will be struck by many booms: probably there will be SSTs overflying

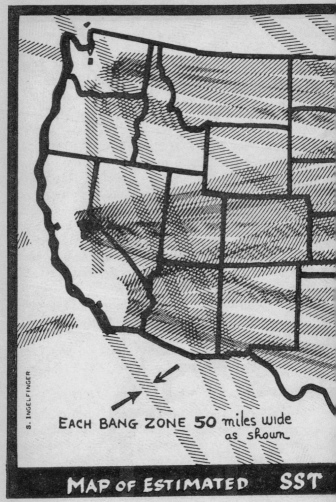

EACH BANG ZONE **50** miles wide
as shown

MAP OF ESTIMATED SST

Figure 5

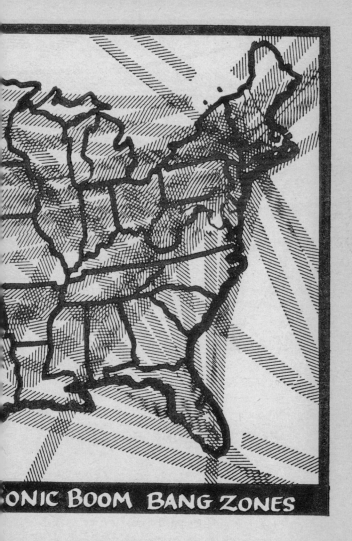

SONIC BOOM BANG ZONES

from other locations more than 100 miles away, and such SSTs' booms will strike it. For example, an SST flying from New York to the southwest might overfly Baltimore, booming it; and an SST from Baltimore might overfly New York, booming *it*.

If one proposes that overflying planes in the vicinity of New York City should always detour (by about 50 miles, presumably) then an enormously increased number of booms would be heard in the nearby cities in New Jersey and Connecticut. This would scarely be fair, and it seems unlikely that Connecticut, say, would willingly accept the booms that New Yorkers were unwilling to endure.

Proposals to detour the metropolitan areas *widely*— so as to pass mainly over sparsely populated regions— would bring outcries from vacationists and nature lovers. National parks and many other vacation areas are sparsely populated; but a concentration of booms in these areas could have devastating effects, as the Sierra Club and the Wilderness Society have already pointed out. (See Chapter 9.)

Annoyance Estimates

How many people would suffer daily annoyance from sonic booms if the SST-builders' dreams come true and 1,800 SSTs are put into use over land and sea? No detailed estimate has been made, but it is highly likely that more than 25 percent of all the people on earth would be involved. On the order of one *billion* persons would be hit by booms.

Some of these would perhaps accept the booms. Probably at least half would find them highly annoying. Among these would be millions of especially vulnerable people (see Chapter 5) who would suffer greatly.

Over-all conclusions as to the annoyance of the sonic boom are presented in Chapter 11.

Damage Payment Dilemma

Some pro-SST persons have said that the sonic boom problem is largely solved if one can arrange to make *prompt* damage payments to the owners of the houses damaged by the booms.

But to arrange fair and prompt damage payments would be virtually impossible, because:

The homeowner will often be unable to prove that his glass, plaster, masonry, etc., was indeed damaged by the boom, and not by ground settlement or other cause.

The homeowner will not be able to find out which airplane, which pilot, which airline, or which nationality of airline was responsible for damage caused at a specified time. The plane is 20 to 40 miles away by the time its boom strikes the house, and is then out of sight.

Damage can be cumulative—a result of booms from many planes over a period of many weeks. Blame for such damage cannot be ascribed to any *one* plane.

The expense of filing a claim for small damage may exceed the amount claimed for the damage.

An agency engaged in evaluating and paying claims may find itself enmeshed in prolonged and bitter disputes with tens of thousands of homeowners every month. Thousands of claims adjusters may be needed, and hundreds of lawyers. Agency and homeowner alike will be relying on circumstantial evidence. Injustice will be frequent, and hard-feeling likewise.

To make damage payments for human annoyance and human suffering from the boom would be fantastically difficult. How can one put a price on a sleepless night? An aggravated headache or ulcer? An irritable mood? A permanent feeling of despair at forever surrendering peace and quiet in the home? One may ask also about a heart patient under doctor's orders to avoid becoming excited or startled, or a house painter who is startled and falls from a ladder, or a nervous and pregnant woman who miscarries as a result of startle effect. An eminent eye-surgeon has already warned that eye-surgeons must not be startled during a delicate eye operation; an involuntary motion of the surgeon's hand might produce permanent blindness (letter of September 12, 1968, by Dr. Henry F. Allen, Director of Post-Graduate Program in Ophthalmology, Harvard Medical School).

How would a museum director collect damages for priceless objets d'art, or archaeological specimens, damaged by broken glass from a museum skylight? How could a symphony orchestra director collect for the harm done to a tape recording of a symphony interrupted by sonic booms? How can a vacation-resort hotel-owner collect for loss of customers who dislike vacationing in a region lying beneath a main SST flight route?

A few of these questions have been broached by the Federal Aviation Administration—and dismissed with remarks to the effect that "some suitable procedure would have to be worked out."

Can a suitable procedure be worked out? For two years Professor W. F. Baxter of the Stanford School of Law studied this problem; late in 1968, in a carefully written 57-page report (B-3), he announced his conclusions:

"The SST will expose so many people to its disturbing and often destructive shock waves that any attempt to account for all those costs, ranging from trivial annoyance to serious physical injury, and to require that the aviation industry pay those costs to those upon whom the costs fortuitously fall would be impossible of accomplishment.

"Present governmental generosity toward the SST program is a discouraging comment on our sense of national priorities: It may soon be possible to fly from Watts to Harlem in 2 hours and to disrupt the lives of everyone in between."

Other lawyers have come to equally discouraging conclusions. R. P. Keller of the Denver University College of Law presented his results in a thesis entitled "Sonic Boom: Legal Misfit." G. K. Gleason, at the Harvard Law School, gave his views in a 162-page thesis "Supersonic Transport and the Sonic Boom." L. A. Huard's views are summarized in his 37-page article, "The Roar, The Whine, The Boom and the Law: Some Legal Concerns about the SST" (H-2).

Representative Seymour Halpern and fourteen associates have called for creation of a Sonic Boom Damage Fund; the Secretary of Transportation would decide how much each airline should contribute, and claims for damage to buildings would be paid from this fund— if the claims were adequately documented. There would be no compensation paid for *annoyance* caused by the booms. Charles M. Haar, Assistant Secretary for Housing and Urban Development, proposed a somewhat different scheme. He would make the airlines pay for the noise they produce: they would lease "air-noise rights" for a period of three years and then make payments proportional to the decrease in property values. In a 1968 seminar conducted by Professor D. Cavers of the Harvard Law School it was proposed that all sonic-boom damage claims be handled by an *international* agency from assessments levied on all pertinent airlines of all the countries concerned. The near impossibility of discovering a fair and efficient procedure was conceded.

What Is an Acceptable Boom?

The question of an *acceptable boom* has been explored at length by the Swedish aeronautics expert B. Lundberg (L-12, L-14, L-16). After weighing the results from all major sonic boom tests made to date, and taking into account unavoidable variations in boom overpressure and the widely varying vulnerability of people, he concludes that a boom having a nominal overpressure of about 0.1 pounds per square foot is about the most intense boom that could be accepted by the population as a whole during the daytime and also at night. During the daytime only, 0.2 psf booms might be acceptable—but it must be remembered that there are many people (night-shift workers, sick persons, infants) who sleep during the daytime.

The predicted overpressures of the SSTs are *ten to thirty times* the generally acceptable value 0.1 psf adopted by Lundberg.

In the U.S.A., Professor R. L. Bauer, Chairman of the Subcommittee on Human Response, Committee on SST-Sonic Boom, National Academy of Sciences, reviewed the available information and concluded that the acceptable limit was probably well below 0.75 psf (B-2). He gave consideration to adopting a value as low as 0.2 psf, but declined to designate any specific value. Pro-SST persons have been reticent as to what boom intensity is acceptable, perhaps because they wish to leave open the possibility that whatever intensity the SSTs actually produce can, somehow, be declared acceptable.

Is There a Cure for the Boom?

There is a clear consensus among experts that there is no "cure"—even dimly in sight—for the sonic boom. The National Academy of Sciences' Committee on SST-Sonic Boom announced, after a two-year study led by Dr. Raymond L. Bisplinghoff, Dean of Aeronautics at

M.I.T., that ". . . future prospects for dramatic reduction in the intensities of sonic boom produced by supersonic aircraft are not readily apparent" (N-1). Dr. A. J. Evans, NASA Director of Sonic Boom Research, stated that ". . . it's becoming obvious that the sonic boom will probably be unacceptable over land" (*Business Week,* October 18, 1967). Various technical studies by NASA have shown that there is no cure in sight for the sonic boom (U-17). Dr. D. Hornig, White House Director of Science and Technology, told a House subcommittee on February 28, 1968, that ". . . no major breakthrough can be expected in the foreseeable future" (*Aviation Daily,* March 1, 1968).

In a 280-page Congressional staff report (L-3) it has been stated that "The sonic boom is an inescapable by-product of forcing any large, heavy object through the air at speeds greater than the velocity of sound."

Thus the consensus is that the sonic boom is to be regarded as a "fact of nature." Ocean-going ships create large bow waves, and have done so since time immemorial. No cure has been found. The sonic boom of an SST is in the same category.

The sonic boom depends partly on the lift required to keep the plane in the air, i.e., on the weight of the plane. It depends also on the detailed design of the plane—its configuration and streamlining. It is generally agreed that the sonic-boom component due to the weight of the plane is unavoidable: it cannot be circumvented (unless the plane slows down to subsonic speed—or rises so high it is above the atmosphere!) The component that depends on streamlining can be reduced by making the plane longer and more slender; but the existing designs are already so long and slender that stability, maneuverability, and passenger space are disappointing.

There have been various claims of partial "cures," but these have turned out to be without real merit.

Early in 1967 Northrup engineers proposed that an intense electrical discharge be maintained somehow just in front of the leading edge of the wing, and along the entire length of the wing, to heat the air there and start it moving out of the way before it is struck by the on-coming wing. But the idea seems impractical in many ways: *acres* of ionization would be required each second, an enormous power plant would be needed to generate the high-voltage electricity, an enormous electrode system would be needed, there would be danger from having electrical flashes so close to (possibly leaky) fuel tanks in the wings. Also there would be much added weight, and widespread interference with radio and TV signals received in the houses below. William T. Hamilton, a top Boeing executive, has declared the scheme to be "impractical" (*Electronic News,* January 29, 1968). Other Boeing engineers have declared the scheme would require 1,000 megawatts of electrical power, enough for a large city! (*Aviation Week,* February 3, 1969). Dean R. L. Bisplinghoff, M.I.T. aeronautics expert, has called the scheme ". . . untenable" (*Technology Review,* May 1968, p. 61).

Likewise the suggestion by Dr. Edwin L. Resler of Cornell's School of Aerospace Engineering proved to be of academic interest only. He proposed that the incipient shockwave be somehow "swallowed" by the airplane engines and dissipated harmlessly. But no workable scheme for funneling the shockwave into the engines has been proposed, and the FAA has declared this system also to be of no practical significance (letter of April 4, 1968, by C. L. Blake, Chief, Engineering Division, SST Development, FAA). *Aviation Daily* for July 1, 1968, implies that Resler's idea could not be made practical for at least 20 years.

Palliatives exist, but are of limited effectiveness. Take

the choice of altitude, for example. If the cruising altitude of an SST is increased, the boom overpressure at ground level decreases. However, the decrease is disappointingly small: it varies approximately as the first power (not the square!) of the altitude. More exactly, it varies approximately as

$$(\text{altitude})^{3/4}$$

as shown by Carlson and McLain in *International Science and Technology* (C-1). In any event, the SSTs are already scheduled to fly at enormous altitude (55,000 to 70,000 feet, where the density of the air is only about 6 percent that at sea level); and even when at these altitudes, they would produce, at ground level, boom intensities of about 2.0 to 3.5 pounds per square foot.

As the fuel in an SST is gradually consumed (at the rate of ½ to 1 ton per minute, during the early part of the trip) the plane becomes lighter and the boom overpressure decreases somewhat, becoming about 10 to 20 percent less at the end of the supersonic flightpath.

In mid-1969 Lockheed engineers proposed a "theoretical" scheme for reducing the prevalence of sonic booms. They pointed out that if an SST flies *barely* above the speed of sound (at Mach 1.15, say), if it flies at high altitude (above 40,000 feet), if the air is free of turbulence, and if the air near the ground is especially warm, the portion of the shock wave traveling toward the ground will curve forward and may actually miss the earth. Typically, there *is* turbulence; thus the scheme would fail frequently. In any event, such a "slow SST" would have little appeal to the airlines.

A light (smaller) SST would have a less intense boom than a large SST, other things being equal. But the economics of building and flying small SSTs, with small passenger capacity, become unfavorable, and the annoyance produced on the ground *per passenger carried* may actually increase.

Chapter 7

Dangers in SST Flight

Fire

The SST will carry a far greater fuel load than any earlier type of air transport. The fuel load of the Boeing SST at take-off will be almost 200 tons. Much of the fuel will be stored in the wings; many different tanks will be used; the tanks are to be interconnected by large numbers of pipes, valves, and an elaborate system of pumps for transferring fuel from one tank to another, to maintain balance of the plane. The leading edges of the wings will become very hot—about 500 or even 500° F in some instances (W-1, p. 108).

The Federal Aviation Administration's worries as to fire are evident in its 200-page "Tentative Airworthiness Standards for Supersonic Transports," January, 1969, (U-13). On page 99 one finds:

"A broader safety problem exists, arising from the presence of ignitable fuel-air mixtures in the tanks and venting systems. Possible sources of ignition are: electrostatic discharges, unusual lightning strikes, ground fires, unforeseen arcing and sparking from electrical components, and hot metal fragments from engine disintegration. This potential fire and explosion hazard is not unique to the SST; however, it represents a safety threat which is more critical for the SST because of the broad fuel temperature ranges likely to be experienced, and the greater quantities of fuel stored in or near the fuselage areas."

On pages 100-104 one finds:

"Means must be provided for preventing or suppressing fire and explosion within the fuel tanks and venting systems in the presence of ignition sources from fire, friction heat, and electrical arcs and sparks, under all conditions of ground and flight operation including servicing.

". . . FAA concern over the variety of forms of potential ignition sources and what appears to be a lack of good information for controlling these sources was discussed.

". . . It is fairly clear at this point that titanium or stainless steel will be used for fuselage skin. Both of these have high friction sparking tendencies.

". . . In the case of pressurized tanks, there is the possibility that fuel will be sprayed out through an opening in a damaged tank or line or through the vent system in the event of a crash landing . . ."

On page 104 the danger of fire in empty spaces between fuel tanks is discussed:

"Spaces may exist, for instance, in the leading edges of wings where high temperatures will prevail as a result of aerodynamic heating. Spaces may exist under fuselage tanks if the tanks are elevated to protect them from possible damage during a wheels-up landing. In the event of such a landing, scraping action would produce both heat and sparks. Other sources of ignition could originate from equipment located in the space or from punctures in the skin where temperatures up to the stagnation temperature might occur. It is extremely difficult to prevent all leaks . . . fuel leakage into areas surrounding fuel storage is frequently encountered in service."

Engine fires, too, are a threat. On pages 121 and 122 the feasibility of extinguishing engine fires is discussed:

"The capability to shut off the flow of flammable fluids will be even more important in the case of the SST because an engine fire occurring during high-Mach flight will be difficult, if not impossible, to extinguish with extinguishing agent. Engine and cowl surfaces at these high speeds will reignite a fire if flow continues.

"In the supersonic airplane, there may be a need for protection not only against burn-through but against radiation effects which may be of sufficient magnitude to affect other parts of the airplane or to initiate fires on the protected side of the firewall . . .

". . . Because fires may be more difficult to extinguish during supersonic flight and may persist for extended periods until airspeed and altitude can be reduced, protection must also be provided against prolonged exposure to radiation generated by a fire."

Hail

Subsonic planes, traveling at 300 to 500 mph, have been seriously damaged on encountering hailstones one or two inches in diameter, as indicated in many technical reports (for example, World Meteorological Organization *Technical Note 89,* V-1). For an SST to enter a region of hail is far more serious because of the greater speed of the plane; the velocity of the hailstones relative to the airplane is far greater than the speed of an ordinary .22-rifle bullet. The SST flies very high, but hail is occasionally present at altitudes greater than 65,000 feet (D-1, p. 80).

The FAA's worries concerning hail have been stated clearly enough (U-13, pp. 177, 178). Discussing possibilities of SSTs colliding with birds and hailstones, FAA engineers stated:

"The most critical of such materials at supersonic speeds is likely to be hailstones. A review of meteorological literature on hailstone observations and theory of development indicates that little reliable information is available concerning what sizes and densities can be expected in the high altitudes. One difficulty is that of determining hail size in the air. There is ample evidence that hailstones occur at high altitudes, with convective cloud tops up to 70,000 feet. Over an eight-year period, USAF aircraft are reported to have experienced 272 damaging hail encounters. Forty-six percent of these encounters occurred above 20,000 feet, with maximum height at 44,000 feet. Pilots have reported hailstones of possibly three to five inches between 29,000 and 37,000 feet.

"At the October 1967 FAA/Industry meeting, it was commented that strikes are being reported in spite of weather radar and that we should test larger hail sizes, up to five inches . . . FAA feels that testing with fewer than actual concentrations will establish the strength to resist impact, as multiple strikes at the same spot are unlikely . . . For engines it is felt that minor damage from two-inch stones would be acceptable."

The FAA has called for sufficient tests ". . . to assure that (1) encounter of large size (e.g., 4-inch diameter) hail, and (2) encounter of hail at higher speeds (e.g., speed associated with 50,000 feet cruise Mach number) will not result in catastrophic structural failure."

Lightning

J. D. Robb of the Lightning and Transients Research Institute has indicated that titanium provides a definite lightning risk—more so than aluminum. In his article in *Aviation Week* of November 13, 1967, he says that tests employing artificial lightning have demonstrated this fact. Further information may be found in World Meteorological Organization *Technical Note No. 89* (W-1).

Some aluminum planes have fallen victim to lightning. An example is cited in an *Associated Press* release of May 4, 1968:

Dawson, Tex.—Federal authorities waded through ankle-deep mud Saturday seeking to confirm eyewitness reports that lightning may have caused the nation's first major airline crash this year in the loss of a Braniff International Electra and all 84 persons aboard.

The four-engined turboprob airliner, decorated in a

rainbow motif, exploded and fell to earth on an abandoned farm Friday near this central Texas village.

David White, a carpenter, said he saw lightning strike the plane Friday as he worked on a barn. "I thought, I wonder why he's flying right into that storm, and then there was a big flash of lightning. It looked like it went right through the plane. Then it burst into flames and went behind trees."

The explosion of an SST carrying almost 200 tons of kerosene could cause widespread damage to a city below. The explosion danger may be enhanced inasmuch as the fuel is stored in many different parts of the plane and various nearby metallic surfaces are already at high temperature.

At cruising altitude, an SST would be high above most lightning storms. But during the long climb and long descent it might well encounter lightning storms.

In "Lightning Strike Threat Increases," (*Aviation Week,* January 6, 1969) it is stated that a lightning stroke passing through the fuselage can cause ". . . arcing wherever there is poor electrical contact between two adjoining pieces of metal. If this occurs inside the fuel tanks, it can cause explosion and fire."

The FAA's concern is indicated in its statement in the October 1969 Congressional *Hearings* (U-5, p. 260):

"Because of the low thermal and electrical conductivity of titanium, there has been concern that, in the event of a lightning strike, burn-through of the structure or high heating of a fuel tank wall could result in an explosion. This problem has been recognized by Boeing and the FAA . . ."

Clear Air Turbulence

When a subsonic plane enters a region in which a sudden upward stream of air is encountered, or a sequence of upward and downward streams, the sudden forces on the wings are enormous, the wings may bend by a foot or two (measured at the tips), and the plane may temporarily find itself in a dive or climb. Passengers not strapped into their seats may strike their heads on the ceiling of the cabin; severe injury may result.

In some instances airplanes have been literally torn apart. "Extreme turbulence" was the cause of the crash of a Braniff airliner in Nebraska on August 6, 1966, according to the National Transportation Safety Board. The turbulence caused structural failure. The Board said that turbulence ". . . may be more critical today than in the past" because of higher speeds and other factors (*Aviation Daily,* May 16, 1968). Accounts of many other disasters are summarized by Dwiggins (D-1, p. 100).

Some turbulent regions may be seen well ahead of time by the pilot, and he may be able to detour around them. But some severe turbulence occurs in clear air ("clear air turbulence," or CAT), and the plane may plunge into such a region without warning. At altitudes of about 55,000 to 65,000 feet, where SSTs will cruise, CAT regions have been found to be surprisingly numerous, according to investigations made with military supersonic planes. XB-70 pilots have found turbulence in 7.2 percent of the over-U.S.A. mileage flown at 40,-000 to 60,000 feet altitude, and in 3.3 percent of the mileage over 65,000 feet. (Report NASA-TN-D-4209.) According to the FAA (U-5, p. 259) clear air turbulence can be encountered at any altitude and is one third as intense at 60,000 feet as at 20,000 feet.

SSTs, with their exceptionally high speed, are especially vulnerable to sudden accelerations and strains from CAT. Many pages are devoted to the subject in a recent World Meteorological Organization report (W-1); see also "Clear Air Turbulence," Y. H. Pao and A. Goldburg, Consultants Bureau, New York 1969

(P-1). The higher speed of the SST, the thinner profiles of the wings, the poor visibility, and poor maneuverability all conspire to make CAT a major threat.

Poor Visibility

Traveling at 1,800 mph, a Boeing SST would cover one mile in two seconds, and 10 miles in 20 seconds. If atmospheric conditions limit a pilot's vision to less than 10 miles, he can see no farther ahead than the distance to be traveled in the next 20 seconds. The angular width of vision is limited also. In moderate haze the pilot may be flying virtually blind. Persons who know that hundreds of near-misses occur each year in crowded airspace, and know that occasional fatal collisions occur, find this prospect unpleasant. In 1966, pilots reported 462 near-misses, and the true number has been estimated at 5,000 per year (C-2). In 1968 a total of 2,230 near mid-air collisions were reported, according to the FAA (*Aviation Week*, October 6, 1969).

Poor visibility has been blamed for one of the world's most dramatic airplane crashes—the June 8, 1966, crash of the unique, 250-ton supersonic bomber XB-70 piloted by Al White. The crash was described in detail in the *Life* of November 11, 1966, and the February 1967 *Reader's Digest*: "With limited vision from inside the XB-70's long, reptilian nose, White could not watch the other planes . . ." A photographic plane collided gently with the XB-70, then ". . . pitched upward, rolled sharply to the left and somersaulted . . . slicing the big plane's two vertical fins." The XB-70 turned upside down, and ". . . a big piece of the left wing broke off." The XB-70 struck the ground. It ". . . made a terrible explosion and an enormous plume of smoke came up."

Poor Maneuverability

Being about as long as a football field, the Boeing

SST may be difficult to maneuver To bank the plane and make a slight turn may take many seconds, during which time the plane may have traveled many miles. Sudden avoidance of an obstacle a few miles ahead may be a virtual impossibility. Dodging lightning storms or regions of hail or turbulence ten miles ahead may also be impossible. To turn the plane in a half-circle at cruising speed will require a region about 100 miles wide.

The pilot lacks much of the prompt "feel" that is so important in flying small planes. Great reliance must be placed on electrical equipment.

Loss of Air Pressure in Cabin

In a subsonic plane, if cabin pressure is lost while at moderate altitude, crew and passengers don oxygen masks and suffer no harm. But in an SST, the situation is quite different: the altitude is so great (about 65,000 feet), and the outside air pressure there is so low, that should the plane lose its pressure, sudden "boiling of the blood" would occur, producing unconsciousness of crew and passengers within about one minute. Oxygen masks would not avail. A disastrous crash would be unavoidable. Loss of pressure would occur, for example, if several windows of the plane were to be blown out, or a small bomb blew a hole a few feet in diameter in the side of the plane. The air-pressure-maintenance system is designed to maintain at least a barely livable pressure if a *small* opening (one-foot diameter or less) occurs in the side of the plane, e.g., if one small window is blown out. (U-5, p. 121).

Uncontrolled Temperature Rise in Cabin

Compressing the air to be used in the cabin entails, unavoidably, much adiabatic heating of the air. Elaborate precautions must be taken to cool this air so that crew and passengers will not be killed by "baking" in air as hot as 500° F (*Aeroplane,* May 29, 1968, p. 4). An enormous cooling system, plus an emergency or back-up system, is required. Complete failure of the systems could create serious problems.

Cosmic Radiation

It is not yet known whether intense solar flares from the sun would occur often enough to create a serious problem from high-energy ionizing radiation. According to an article, "Radiobiological Aspects of the Supersonic Transport" (I-3), ionization from cosmic radiation is at a maximum at altitudes of the order of 60,000 to 80,000 feet—just where the SSTs would cruise. The ambient radiation here consists mainly of charged particles (protons, alpha particles, etc.) of very high energy, e.g., many millions of electron volts. A single such particle can do lasting damage to a gene of a human cell. The skin of the plane is not a protection, but just the reverse: it actually causes multiplication of the damaging particles by the process of *shower production.* The radiation levels inside the cabins of SSTs at cruising altitudes are of the order of 100 times what they are at sea level, and amount to 1 or 2 millirems per hour. The usual limit on dose allowed to the public is 500 millirems *per year,* and a limit of 2 millirems per hour is commonly imposed. In the absence of solar flares, the actual level in the SST cabin will usually be just below this limit.

The harmfulness of the cosmic radiation is difficult to predict from laboratory experiments. The cosmic-ray spectrum cannot be duplicated in the laboratory, adequate experimentation on human beings is prohibited, and genetic damage might take decades, or generations, to appear.

It is generally agreed that a dose of such radiation equivalent to 500 *rems* may well prove fatal. The chance that a solar flare might produce a dose of the order of 1 to 20 rems cannot at present be ruled out. Governmental regulations are such that if an SST at high altitude were to receive a dose of 15 rems or more, the pilots and passengers would be advised not to risk receiving additional doses in that year, i.e., advised not to participate in high-altitude SST flights for many months. The economic waste of grounding an SST pilot, whose training for SST flight might represent an investment of the order of $60,000, is obvious (I-2).

It is well established that any high-energy radiation that is unnecessary should be avoided. This is true of all persons, and is especially true of pregnant wo.nen. The human foetus, particularly during the first few weeks of pregnancy when that condition is usually not known, can be seriously damaged by a very small dose of radiation; even a 1-rem dose presents an appreciable risk. It has therefore been suggested that women of childbearing age might be advised to avoid such high-altitude flights. SST hostesses, likewise, should perhaps be beyond childbearing age, and all crew members should be classified as "radiation workers," with their doses and flight-hours controlled accordingly.

Dr S. R. Mohler, Chief, FAA Aeromedical Applications Division, has indicated that SST crews would run the risk that radiation ". . . may shorten the life span by 5 to 10 percent and the gross signs of aging may appear earlier than would otherwise be anticipated." Other possible results of exposure to radiation, according to Dr. Mohler, are damage to sperm cells, bone marrow, lung tissues, kidney tissues, and the lymphatic system—and leukemia. (See also *Astronautics & Aeronautics,* September 1964.)

A pilot could avoid most of the radiation from a solar flare if he were to dive the plane quickly to much lower altitude. The hazards of such an unannounced dive into perhaps already crowded airspace are obvious and the sonic boom damage (from such a low-flying supersonic craft) might be impressive (I-3, W-1, M-1, R-1).

Ozone Danger

Special precautions must be taken to eliminate active ozone from the cabin of the SSTs. Ozone exists naturally at high altitude, and it is now known that even extremely small concentrations (of the order of one part per million) are dangerous (W-1).

According to the FAA: "Atmospheric ozone concentrations at SST cruising altitudes are several times greater than the maximum permissible cabin ozone concentrations . . . Ozone contamination following system malfunctions may be an added hazard concerning SST cabin environmental control (U-13).

Metal Fatigue at High Temperature

The early British Comet planes suffered disasters because of metal fatigue. In the SSTs, fatigue is especially troublesome because of the extreme flexibility of the structures, the enormous forces produced when flying through bumpy air, and the fact that some of the metal parts are at very high temperature (from the impacting supersonic airflow). Also, big temperature differentials exist: some parts very hot, nearby parts cold, with resulting thermal-expansion strains superimposed on other kinds of strain. It is impossible to make adequate laboratory studies on such combinations of sudden flexures and high and non-uniform temperatures; thousands of hours of actual flight through turbulent air—even several years of testing—would be necessary to provide assurance that metal fatigue, shortened useful life, and perhaps sudden disaster will not occur. Because drastically new metal fabrication methods are used, and new structural arrangements, practical experience is, at this stage, meagre. It is already well known that the aluminum alloy Hiduminium RR 58 used in the Concorde ". . . gradually loses its strength from the cumulative effects of heating" (*New Scientist,* May 9, 1968, p. 285). See also *Aerospace Technology,* May 20, 1968.

The FAA has stated that ". . . it is extremely difficult to assure that fatigue cracking of the (SST) structure will not occur in service or to predict where it will occur." Also ". . . landing and take-off loading conditions may be critical for significant portions of SST flight structure such as the fuselage. Failure of such structure during these high speed ground conditions could be catastrophic." (U-13, pp. 65-66).

The Air Force's C-130 mammoth cargo planes have already been plagued with metal fatigue and weakening of the wings (*New York Times,* November 26, 1968).

High Landing Speed

The most dangerous part of flying is the landing, and the actual landing speed is an important factor. Experience with many kinds of planes has shown that, other things being comparable, the hazard increases with the 3rd power of the landing speed. Thus increasing the landing speed by 50 percent may be expected to increase the hazard by a factor of roughly $(1.50)^3$ or about 3.4.

The SSTs are to have very high landing speeds (about 180 mph; see Chapter 2) and the landing operation is expected to be particularly hazardous (L-4 and also *Aeroplane,* December 6, 1967).

Another worrisome fact is that, at touchdown, the pilot sits so high above ground (about 35 feet) that exact visual judgment of height-above-ground just prior to touchdown is difficult. The pilot's height is comparable to that of a man on the fourth floor of an office building.

Inability to "Hold" for Long Periods

Subsonic planes, using relatively little fuel per hour, can hold for hours near a crowded airport, awaiting permission to land. If the chosen airport is closed because of a storm or an accident, the subsonic plane can fly to some other airport—perhaps 500 or 1,000 miles away, if necessary. But the SST uses on the order of a half ton of fuel per minute, and can ill afford to take off with any greater reserve of fuel than is absolutely necessary. Thus its ability to hold over an airport, or to be diverted to a distant airport, is restricted. The Concorde's fuel reserve guaranteed by the manufacturer —for flight from Paris to New York—is only ". . . 30 minutes over alternate" and ". . . this appears unrealistic" because of the need to hold during congestion at peak load times (*Aeroplane,* April 17, 1968).

Limited Number of Airports Available in Emergency

Because SSTs require very long runways and specially strengthened surfaces (to take the enormous weight and landing impact), relatively few airports can accept an SST. Thus the number of secondary, or emergency, landing sites is small. The Boeing SST will require 10,300 feet (almost two miles) for take-off (*Hearings,* U-5, p. 30).

Incompatibility with Other Kinds of Planes

With its high speed, high altitude of cruise, poor maneuverability, and limited fuel reserves, the SST is in many ways poorly compatible with, or incompatible with, other types of planes—as regards routes, headway separations, holding patterns, landing priorities (U-5, p. 234), and other obvious categories such as pilot training and airplane servicing. Extra expense and perhaps extra danger may be involved (*Aviation Week,* October 24, 1968, pp. 149 and 153).

Pilot Strain

The strain on the SST pilot will be enormous. The number of tasks he must perform, their novelty, and the requisite speed of execution are impressive. Even on conventional transport planes the strain is great. In 1966 there were six instances in which a pilot on duty on the flight deck of a commercial plane suffered sudden incapacitation from cardiovascular disease (*Aviation Daily,* December 22, 1967). In the last eight years, 14 commercial transports crashed during training flights. The strain on an SST pilot must be exceptionally great: he is handling a more cumbersome and complicated plane, relying on a greater array of automatic (and often invisible) equipment, with need for quicker decisions. Presumably he will be well aware that a crash may mean loss of a $50,000,000 plane, liability for perhaps $60,-000,000 in lawsuits by the heirs of the victims, and glaring publicity throughout much of the world.

Inadequate Testing

When testing small planes, produced at reasonable cost, a test pilot can put the plane through its paces with gusto. Besides trying out all the recommended flight conditions and maneuvers, he can try some extra-curricular tests, such as flying through bad storms, diving steeply, stalling, landing cross-wind, or deliberately making a hard landing with exaggerated bounce. He can find whether the plane holds up well even when abused.

But the SST pilot, realizing that the prototype plane may be worth $250,000,000 and that to build a replacement would take a year or two, must be careful *not* to make the extreme tests that would be of such interest.

If some design error is found in a small plane, the manufacturer can modify the design quickly and produce and test additional planes. But to modify an SST could be a major undertaking, slowing down the whole program by months or years and causing large financial loss.

Sabotage

From time to time airplanes have been sabotaged by persons with a grudge against some passenger, or persons hoping to collect the life-insurance on some passenger. When such a plane crashes, the pieces can often be reassembled to show where and how the disaster occurred, and the guilty person may be caught. But supersonic SST flight may be permitted just over the oceans; thus if an SST is sabotaged, the disaster will occur over the ocean and the plane will crash and sink, perhaps with little or no evidence remaining as to what caused the disaster, and little chance of finding the guilty person. Merely blowing a three-foot hole in the cabin wall, or bursting an outer door, would reduce the air pressure drastically and crew and passengers would die almost instantly. The radio operator might not survive long enough to send off a message as to the cause of the disaster; thus the cause might forever remain a mystery. In addition to the tragic deaths of passengers and crews, there would be substantial financial loss. Even a single such crash—unexplained—might cause the public to shy away from SSTs, and might cause the regulatory agencies to ground all SSTs pending prolonged inquiry.

Expected Number of Crashes

"Qualified observers . . . foresee the loss of two B-747 jumbo jets during the first eighteen months . . . after that plane becomes operational," according to the Washington, D.C. Insurance News Letter, Inc. (*New York*

Times, September 15, 1968; see also *Astronautics & Aeronautics* of April 1968). This estimate is based on past experience with new types of airplanes. The SST, having far more radical design features than the jumbo jet, may be expected to have an even more ominous record in the first years of service.

Chapter 8

Discomforts in SST Flight

Minor Discomforts

SSTs will cut several hours off the typical travel time between American and European cities, but they will do so at the price of several discomforts.

Space will be at a premium in the SST. There will be but one aisle, and the general roominess will be inferior to that of the jumbo jet.

The mandatory seat-belts-fastened time will be much greater. Initial acceleration to cruising speed will take of the order of 20 minutes, and the later deceleration likewise. The greater threat from turbulence, including unpredictable turbulence, may entail greater use of seatbelts during the cruise. The FAA recommendation (U-5, p. 261) is ". . . to keep the seatbelt loosely fastened at all times when seated."

Turbulence may bother SST passengers more than subsonic-plane passengers, according to a study made by A. J. Kantor, Aerospace Instrumentation Laboratory, Air Force Cambridge Research Laboratories, Hanscom Field, Massachusetts. Subsonic planes "ease slowly" into successive up- or down-currents of air, and accordingly the passengers experience, typically, vertical accelerations of only 0.1 g. But an SST, traveling at three times the speed of a subsonic jet, may be subjected to accelerations of 0.2 to 0.3 g. which, judged by experience over many years, may cause the passengers noteworthy discomfort. (*Washington Scientific Trends,* June 2, 1969).

The acceleration at start of climb will be greater than in typical jets and the cabin floor will be at a much steeper angle at that time. Acceleration will continue for a longer time—10 to 20 minutes.

The windows are so small as to be little more than peep-holes. Passengers must resign themselves to seeing virtually nothing of the landscape, seascape, or cloud formations below. Persons prone to claustrophobia may suffer.

Other Drawbacks

SSTs are so expensive that few standby planes will be available. If an SST develops mechanical trouble just before scheduled departure time, a very long delay may ensue. Mechanical or electrical trouble is relatively likely to occur because of the enormous number of highly complex instruments and controls involved. Careful repair is essential because of the catastrophic dangers that could result from malfunction of equipment.

The variety of SST routes and take-off times will be few, relative to great variety afforded by the jumbo jets and other subsonic planes. It is expected that by the time a few Boeing SSTs are in use there will be about 450 jumbo jets in use. The SSTs may be confined to overwater routes, whereas the jumbo jets can fly equally well over land or water.

Long-distance SST trips across time-zones will give the traveler little chance to adjust his "biological clock," or circadian rhythm. Many kinds of biological and psychological disruptions may occur (*Science,* June 13, 1969, p. 1288). Many corporation executives who fly from continent to continent are not allowed to make a major decision until after they have spent 48 hours in the country of arrival. "Air travelers who cross the . . .

Pacific . . . generally suffer a desynchronization of certain biological rhythms. Their timing mechanism "goes awry" (*Parade,* Januuary 14, 1968, p. 20). Dr. S. R. Mohler, Chief of Medical Applications, FAA, says " . . . allow one or two days' acclimatization before taking part in demanding activities . . ." Thus the primary benefit of the SST—the saving in time—is diminished.

On a typical SST flight, most passengers will get no sleep. On nighttime flights this will be a major embarrassment. Consider a traveler who leaves New York at 11:00 p.m. bound for London. He will reach his hotel in London at about 3:30 a.m. New York time, which is 8:30 a.m. London time—just as the working day there begins. But he will have had no sleep!

Is it practical to give up such nighttime flights and fly the Atlantic just during the day? Certainly not, not only because the traveler then wastes the better part of the day en route, but also because the small chance that SST operation might be profitable disappears entirely unless the SSTs are kept in use almost constantly, night and day (U-5).

Chapter 9

Degradation of Environment

Take-Off Noise

It is estimated that the SSTs will produce, in areas off to the side of the take-off path, an engine roar far louder than that of today's biggest commercial planes. Even pro-SST persons who try to belittle the sonic boom admit that the engine roar at take-off will be a major problem. Boeing's concern is well known (*Aerospace Technology,* May 20, 1968, p. 53). President Nixon's *SST ad hoc Review Committee* (P-4, p. H-10435) has pointed out that the Boeing SST's engines "are fundamentally noisier than the fan engines that are optimum for the subsonic jets." A Swiss airline official has said: "I am deeply worried about the SST's sideline noise during take-off . . . populated areas *abreast of the runway* will be flooded with noise that exceeds today's noise level, generated by DC-8's and 707's, by a very, very wide margin" (A. Baltensweiler, Swissair, in *Air Travel Official Airline Guide* of February 1968, p. 14). R. L. Bisplinghoff, former Dean of Aeoronautics at Massachusetts Institute of Technology, has stated: " . . . where the SST is noisier than other airplanes is in its sideline noise . . . here we are definitely over anything that is now flying and we have no immediate prospect of reducing this to the level of the current subsonic jets" (Congressional *Hearings,* October 9, 1959, U-5, p. 28). According to the October 7, 1968, *Guardian,* the Concorde may be "more than twice as noisy as today's aircraft in terms of lateral noise and, to make matters worse, the lower frequencies of its engines will penetrate indoors more easily."

The engine roar at landing, too, will be great. The Concorde, for example, will land at 180 mph with an upward tilt of 10.8 degrees and *with engines on full.* According to *Aerospace Technology* (of May 20, 1968, p. 53), the Concorde "may show a rather startling 124 PNdb figure during approach, primarily because its engine inlets cannot be choked." (The symbol *PNdB* stands for *perceived noise, in decibels.* The decibel is a logarithmic unit. By way of illustration: 50 PNdB corresponds to the amount of noise in a typical quiet living room, 90 PNdB corresponds to the noise beside an expressway on which trucks are going by at high speed, and 120 PNdB is almost unbearably loud. Reference A-3 discusses loudness terminology in great detail.)

What loudness is acceptable? In January of 1969 the FAA circulated a proposed regulation (Docket 9337, Notice 69-1) suggesting an ideal goal (ceiling on noise at airport) of 80 EPNdB and proposing to limit noise of the very heavy (600,000 lb.) subsonic planes to about 108 EPNdB. (The distinction between PNdB and EPNdB is slight, and too technical to explain here.) Specific regulations were being prepared for release prior to the end of 1970.

Strong doubts were expressed in March of 1969 by President Nixon's *SST ad hoc Review Committee* (see Appendix 4) as to whether the Boeing SST could conform to reasonable standards of noise. The Committee indicated that the noise might well be excessive and could cause various adverse effects, including some or all of these: hearing loss, cardiovascular and neurologic changes, and glandular and respiratory troubles. It concluded that ". . . significant numbers of people will file complaints and resort to legal action, and . . . a very high percentage of the exposed population will find the noise intolerable."

How would an airport noise level of 124 PNdB compare with a proposed limit of 108 PNdB, or 80 PNdB? By consulting a table of logarithms, one finds that 124 and 108 PNdB represent a *ratio of 40 to 1*. Thus it would take forty planes of 108 PNdB rating—all taking off at once—to equal the noise of one 124 PNdB SST. How about 124 vs. the ideal goal of 80? It would take 25,000 planes of 80 PNdB rating, all taking off at once, to equal the noise of one 124 PNdB SST.

That the regulatory agencies can permit such engine roar at airports is hard to believe, inasmuch as the trend of recent Congressional action has been to *reduce* airport noise. On July 24, 1968, President Johnson signed bill HR-3400 authorizing and requesting the FAA to set satisfactory limits on such noise. Many Congressmen cited the agony of suburbanites living near airports and pleaded for establishment of lower limits on noise. Court actions, too, have recently favored outright reduction in airport noise—or making substantial damage payments to the persons affected. Total damage claims, because of intolerable airplane take-off and landing noise, by persons living close to Los Angeles International Airport now exceed $5 *billion,* according to *Aviation Daily* of January 31, 1969.

If SSTs are denied permission to land at airports close to cities and are diverted to airports far out in the country, travelers may prefer to travel by jumbo jets and other planes that can use the more convenient, close-in airports.

Pollution Near Airports

At take-off time the Boeing SST would burn about one ton of fuel each minute—far more than subsonic jets burn. The amounts of toxic pollutants inflicted on the nearby downwind communities would be large. Already the people in such communities find such pollution a major annoyance.

Contamination of Upper Atmosphere

Dr. V. J. Schaefer, world-famous atmospheric physicist and Director of Atmospheric Sciences Research Center at Albany, New York, worries lest a fleet of SSTs, discharging on the order of 150,000 tons of water vapor *daily* (from fuel combustion) into the upper atmosphere, produce "global gloom" (*This Week,* August 11, 1968, p. 4). The President's *SST ad hoc Review Committee* (P-4, p. H-10436) believes that by raising the humidity in the upper atmosphere, the SSTs ". . . would alter the radiation balance and thereby possibly affect the general circulation of atmospheric components."

Effects on Animals

It is certain that the SSTs' repeated sonic booms would annoy many kinds of animals. It is *possible* that harmful long-term effects will occur also. There are already many instances in which booms from military planes have caused horses and cows to panic. In Switzerland a herd of prize cattle stampeded over a cliff when frightened by a sonic boom (*National Parks Magazine,* March, 1968), and it is also reported that in France a horse was startled by a boom and ran away, throwing and killing the rider. At the Edwards Air Force Base sonic boom tests, several horses exhibited fright symptoms (N-5).

Mink are especially vulnerable. In 1966, sonic booms from Air Force F-101 jet planes resulted in the death of approximately 2,000 baby mink on the farm of Mr. Z. Taylor of Frazee, Minnesota, according to a finding by the Federal District Court in St. Paul on June 29,

1968. Mr. Taylor was awarded $37,490 damages (*North Shore News,* Bothell, Washington, September 11, 1968; also personal communication). Mink ranchers in Minnesota testified that when sonic booms struck their farms, the female mink ". . . jumped from their boxes, then bounced back into the boxes again. Dead mink kits were found in the boxes and cages afterwards, some of them partially devoured."

Sonic boom tests carried out on mink farms in Virginia in 1967 by the U.S. Department of Agriculture showed that even relatively mild simulated sonic booms (average overpressure 1.0 psf) inflicted on whelping female mink throughout the whelping period resulted in doubling the mortality rate of the baby mink. The mortality rate was 15.5 percent, as compared to 7.2 percent for the control group (U-7).

Chickens and turkeys are startled by sonic booms. Investigators at Edwards Air Force Base reported that chickens and turkeys hit by booms exhibited ". . . pandemonium" (N-5). A farmer in Hallock, Minnesota, was paid $50 because booms caused his chickens to panic and suffocate against a wall (R-1).

Sonic booms may have disastrous effects on colonies of birds that nest on cliffs—because booms make the birds fly off so impetuously that they knock their eggs out of the nest and the eggs then roll or fall and are soon broken. Likewise, eggs can be knocked out of nests in trees. Mass breakage of eggs after sudden loud noises is already well known, according to A. H. Morgan, Executive Vice-President, Massachusetts Audubon Society (letter of December 7, 1968).

U.S.A. and Canadian experts on fish ecology have stated that virtually nothing is known as to whether, or how much, sonic booms might affect fish. It is well known that only an extremely small fraction of the shockwave energy would enter the water, but even this small amount, striking during periods of quiet, might be expected to alarm fish. Fishermen have reported seeing fish—startled by a sonic boom—jump out of the water and then lie on their sides, as if stunned (C-7, p. 21.1). The U.S. Department of the Interior has planned sonic boom tests on fish off the coast of California, but it is hard to see how the booms could be violent enough, and continued throughout a long enough period to represent fairly the long-term disturbance of a fleet of transoceanic SSTs.

Degradation of Park and Wildlife Areas

Secretary of Transportation Alan S. Boyd, testifying before a Congressional Committee on May 22, 1967, said that even if SSTs could not be permitted to fly over densely populated regions (because of the sonic boom), routes over thinly populated areas could probably be worked out. He suggested, for example, that supersonic flights could be permitted between Chicago and the West Coast—an area containing plains, mountains, and few people. Special effort would be made, he implied, to establish SST supersonic routes over such wilderness areas.

But does this make sense? C. Edward Graves, naturalist and writer, says in the Winter 1967-68 *Living Wilderness* (G-3):

> "Imagine a hike or a pack trip into the wildest part of the country in order to enjoy its peculiar characteristics, only to have the quiet of an evening campfire shattered by cannonading booms from the sky! Their unexpectedness is one of the worst features. Tranquility would no longer exist. The nerve-shattering impact upon man, and the harassment to wildlife through constant exposure to the sonic boom, are incalculable."

In a much earlier (1946) *Living Wilderness* article,

Robert Marshall, one of the founders of the Wilderness Society, wrote:

> "The wilderness . . . furnishes unique opportunity for peacefulness and relaxation. A person camping among the remote peaks of the High Sierras or on the source streams of the Flathead River finds no jarring sight or sound, no discordant clash with his instinctive feeling of what is proper. Everything he experiences is in perfect keeping with the wilderness which seems to stretch endlessly around him."

Graves asks:

> "I wonder what Bob would have said about the possibility of a wilderness bombardment by the SSTs by day and by night. To say the least, it would not be in 'perfect keeping with the wilderness.' Perhaps he would have thundered, as he did in his famous 1930 declaration: 'There is just one hope of repulsing the tyrannical ambition of civilization to conquer every niche on the whole earth. That hope is the organization of spirited people who will fight for the freedom of the wilderness.' "

The Wilderness Society has gone on record as urging ". . . that the use of commercial and private aircraft which produce sonic booms which may be heard on the surface of the land be prohibited. On September 9, 1967, the Sierra Club adopted the resolution: "The Sierra Club is opposed to the operation of civil aircraft under conditions that produce sonic booms audible on the surface of the earth."

The writer has received many letters from hikers and campers who have *already* had their national-park vacations partially spoiled by repeated, explosion-like sonic booms from military planes. If SSTs too are allowed to fly at supersonic speed over parks, the number of booms will increase perhaps a hundred-fold.

Are Over-the-Ocean Supersonic Flights Acceptable?

Pro-SST persons regard it as obvious that supersonic flights over oceans are acceptable. The oceans are practically devoid of people, they say; therefore sonic booms present no problems.

But other persons disagree with this. The most eloquent of these is the Swedish aeronautics expert B. Lundberg, who has analyzed the available information and summarized it in his 1968 60-page report "Acceptable Nominal Sonic Boom Overpressure in SST Operation Over Land and Sea" (L-14). Let us list some of the main facts. The greatest concentrations of SST supersonic routes would be over the North Atlantic, between USA and Europe. An SST would produce especially intense booms when carrying an almost full load of fuel during first acceleration above Mach 1; at this time of maximum boom the plane would be just off the coast. But it is just here that the greatest concentrations of freighters, tankers, passenger ships, fishing vessels, and pleasure vessels is highest. Persons on such ships must expect as many as one or two sonic booms per hour, day and night. Worse, they must expect occasional superbooms in the overpressure range 4.0 to 8.0 psf—universally acknowledged to be extremely severe.

Multiple reflections of the boom shockwave from ship superstructures can produce further increase in overpressure. Already investigators of sonic boom effects have observed breakage of a ship's thick plate glass window by a boom that had an estimated overpressure of about 6 psf (L-16; also London *Times,* October, 1969).

How large an area of the North Atlantic would be struck by sonic booms? A surprisingly large area—partly because the east-bound routes and west-bound routes would be spaced about 100 miles apart, and partly because the SSTs would be serving widely scattered cities in the eastern U.S.A. and Canada and equally widely scattered cities in Europe. Bang-zone maps published in the July 1967 *Space Aeronautics* suggest that about 80 percent of the area of the North Atlantic bounded by lines drawn from Newfoundland to Ireland and from New York to Portugal would be blanketed by booms. Keeping the SSTs and ships on well-separated, parallel courses is out of the question because of the many departure points and many destinations of ships as well as SSTs. It has been estimated that each SST flight across the North Atlantic would boom about 4,000 persons, on the average.

It will be strange indeed if shipowners consent to such treatment and if crew members will consent to be treated as second-class citizens, to be subjected to repeated booms considered too severe to be inflicted on people on land.

Yachtsmen, too, may be expected to protest. On July 18, 1969, the Citizens League Against the Sonic Boom released a list of 118 prominent yachtsmen whose objections to coastal sonic booms had been conveyed to President Nixon. Each of the 118 yachtsmen had signed a petition reading:

> "As one who frequents coastal waters of USA, I oppose using these waters as a dumping-ground for sonic booms from SSTs and I respectfully request government authorities to do their best to prevent this degradation of the environment.
> "Should the airlines proceed to inflict sonic booms routinely on these waters, in disregard to my rights there, I will consider taking appropriate legal action to protect those rights."

Many persons regard the oceans as one of man's great assets. They want to preserve a livable environment there. They are not pleased at aviation's intent to reduce the oceans to a sonic boom dumping ground.

Incidentally, SST proponents often forget how many islands there are. If inflicting SSTs' sonic booms on land is banned, the ban would include islands. For the SSTs to circumvent islands is often not feasible—if adjacent

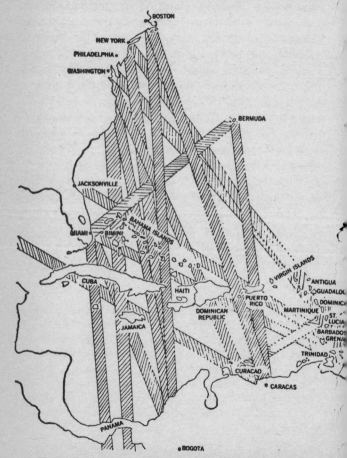

Figure 6—Estimated SST Sonic-Boom Bang-Zones
in Caribbean Area

islands are less than 50 miles apart (because the bang-zone is about 50 miles wide) and form long chains. The 900-mile-long east-west chain of Caribbean islands, for example, would block a majority of the direct routes from the eastern U.S. to South America. (See Figure 6.)

Pro-SST persons, trying to prove that the SSTs *can* be permitted to boom the oceans *ad lib,* point to the fact that military supersonic airplanes have been producing booms at sea for many years—with very few complaints resulting. But they overlook three important facts: (1) The SSTs will be five to ten times heavier than the typical military planes, and will produce far more intense booms. (2) The SSTs would increase the number of booms by a factor of 100. (3) Considerations of national defense (patriotism) will not apply to SSTs carrying businessmen and tourists; the boom victims will see no reason to refrain from complaining. As far as the writer can ascertain, pro-SST groups have never tried to find out whether the hundreds of thousands of persons who spend much of their lives at sea are willing to be boomed night and day, year after year.

Chapter 10

Production, Sales, and Government Hand-Out

Predictions as to production, sales, and financing of the proposed SSTs are highly controversial. SST proponents say that the Boeing SST will cost about $37 million, that there are already 122 orders on hand, and that the terms of the contract between the Government and the manufacturers insure that the Government will get all its money back with interest. But skeptics say that the price will be $50 to $80 billion, there are no firm orders, and there is no assurance the Government will get any money back. Let us consider the available facts.

Price

The Concorde SST, originally expected to cost about $12 million, is now expected to cost at least $21 million (U-5, p. 67).

The Boeing SST is expected by the FAA to cost $37 million in terms of 1967 dollars and about $52 million in terms of dollars that apply when the planes are actually sold (statement by B. J. Vierling, FAA Acting Director of SST Development, U-5, p. 67). A detailed analysis made by the Institute of Defense Analyses, Inc. at the request of the FAA indicates that the price may be $60 to $80 million, especially if supersonic flight over land is banned (I-2).

Orders or Positions

There are no truly firm orders for Concorde or Boeing

SSTs. Rather, various airlines have subscribed to *positions* in what amounts to a waiting line.

There are 74 positions for Concordes:

Eight positions each for Air France, BOAC, Pan Am.
Six positions each for American, Eastern, TWA, United.
Four positions each for Air Canada, Qantas.
Three positions each for Braniff, Continental, Japan, Lufthansa.
Two positions each for Air India, MEA, Sabena.

The total number of positions has remained unchanged for 2½ years, to the embarrassment of the manufacturers.

The casual nature of the positions is indicated by the following statement by Mr. Yves Pratte, President General, Air Canada: "I think I should tell you that Air Canada has not yet ordered any supersonic aircraft. We have line position agreements for four Concordes and six Boeing SSTs and the decision as to the actual purchase of these aircraft will be taken in the light of the most reliable scientific information available at the time the decision is made" (letter of January 28, 1969, to Mr. J. Clare of Toronto).

How many positions have been taken for Boeing SSTs? A Boeing pamphlet of May 1969 presents these numbers:

Fifteen positions for Pan-Am.
Twelve positions for TWA.
Six positions each for Air Canada, Air France, Alitalia, American, BOAC, KLM, Northwest, Qantas, United.
Five positions each for Eastern, Japan Air Lines.
Three positions each for Canadian Pacific, Continental, Delta, Iberia, Lufthansa, World.
Two positions each for Air India, Braniff Interna-

tional, El Al, Irish Air Lines, Pakistan, Trans-
American Aero Corp.
One position for Airlift International.

The total, 122, has remained essentially unchanged
for two years.

In most instances the airlines have made advance
payments of $1 million "risk money" per position. By
September 1969 the total amount of such payments was
$60 million. This is only about 2 percent of the total cost
of the planes involved but provides a minimum factual
basis for the FAA's claim that "the airlines are partici-
pating in the financing."

Financing the Concorde

The British and French governments are financing
the Concorde development, on a 50-50 basis. By the
end of 1969 total expenditures were approximately $1
billion. With three years yet to go, the total cost may
reach $2.5 billion.

Of this, the airlines with positions have contributed
$10 million—less than 1 percent of the total.

Financing the Tu-144

The Soviet Tu-144 is, of course, financed entirely by
the Soviet government.

Financing the Boeing SST

Phases I and II of the U.S. SST Project (preliminary
research, design competition, and preliminary designs)
were completed in 1966 with a total expenditure of $308
million, of which $291 million was paid by the Govern-
ment.

Phase III (completing the design of a prototype SST,
building two such prototypes, and carrying out 100 hours
of flight tests) started in 1967 and is continuing. The

cost of this phase through the end of calendar year 1969 was in the neighborhood of $450 million, of which about 85 percent was provided by the Government. On September 23, 1969, President Nixon requested $96 million for Fiscal Year 1970 and $314, $189, $48, and $15 million for Fiscal Years 1971, 1972, 1973, and 1974, respectively—i.e., $662 million for Fiscal Years 1970 to 1974 inclusive. The total cost of Phase III will amount to $1,339 million, of which the Government will be paying $994 million, the manufacturers $285 million, and the airlines $60 million (*Hearings,* U-5, p. 97). In general, the Government is paying 85 to 90 percent of the expenses of basic type and 75 percent of overrun expenses.

Phase IV (preparation for production, prolonged flight testing, obtaining certification) would commence in mid-1973 if there were no misadventure. The cost is estimated by the FAA at $700 million.

Phase V (start of production) would begin in 1974. The cost is estimated by the FAA at $2.5 billion (*Hearings,* U-5, p. 94).

Critics of the SST program place the costs far higher: $4 to $8 billion in all. They believe the FAA figures to be little more than guesses—and the same view was expressed by members of the President's *SST ad hoc Review Committee* (P-4).

Who is to provide the billions of dollars needed for Phases IV and V? SST proponents say that "Private capital *should* be forthcoming. The aviation industry itself *should* carry the financial load." But experts in the Treasury Department and the Council of Economic Advisers see little chance of this; they expect that, once again, the taxpayers (through the Government) will be asked to provide the bulk of the money.

SST advocates loudly protest calling the Government funding of Phase III a hand-out or subsidy. "This is an

investment," they say. "The contract provides for re-
payment to the Government of every cent invested, with
6 percent interest. By the time the 300th SST is sold,
the Government will have recovered its principal and by
the time the 500th is sold the Government will have
recovered principal and received 6 percent interest on
it."

Critics point out that there is no assurance the Government will get a cent back. There is no assurance any
planes will be sold. Even if 99 are sold, the Government
still may get no money back, because the royalty terms
are sufficiently flexible (see U-5, p. 211) that it may
happen that no royalty is called for until after the 99th
plane has been sold. And, incidentally, the interest rate
specified is far below the rates now current.

Chapter 11

Answering the $64 Billion Question

The question is: *Should our Government push the Boeing SST project and support it with billions of taxpayer dollars?* Let us review the main arguments, pro and con.

Let us start with the question of *need*. Would the SST fill an important need? The proponents say it would. They say that an 1,800 mph SST would reduce the flight time across the North Atlantic from 5½ hours (by jumbo jet) to 2½ hours and would reduce the flight time across the Pacific from 10 hours (by jumbo jet) to 6 hours. This is important, they claim. Much time would be saved by high-paid businessmen, dealings with Europe and the Orient would be facilitated, and international trade and goodwill would flourish.

But what really counts is door-to-door travel time. Traveling by SST instead of jumbo jet, a businessman going from a hotel in New York to a hotel in London would reduce his over-all travel time from 9 hours to 6 hours. Going from a hotel in San Francisco to a hotel in Tokyo he would reduce the over-all travel time from 14 hours to 10 hours. (Note: the jumbo jet can make the trip non-stop, hence can fly a great-circle route. The SST must stop to refuel; detouring to Hawaii to refuel would lengthen the trip by about 900 miles.)

Thus the saving in door-to-door travel time would be only about 30 percent. And this saving would be made at the price of eliminating time for rest and sleep, and complicating the "biological clock" problem. Also, SST fares might be 20 to 40 percent higher than jumbo jet fares. SSTs would be less comfortable than jumbo jets, and less safe.

The saving in time afforded by the SST might be offset by various mundane circumstances such as:

Delays in highway traffic en route to the airport.
Delays at the airport (ticket problems, customs, baggage bottleneck, wait for permission to use runway).
Delays while waiting to land, delays in recovering luggage, delays en route to hotel.

Consider next the question of *routes*. The choice of SST routes available to travelers would be small compared to the choice of jumbo jet routes—because the SSTs, with their inevitable sonic booms, could not be permitted to fly at supersonic speed over land (and when flying at *sub*sonic speed their efficiency would be poor and their over-all economics especially poor). Supersonic flight over islands (across the Caribbean chain of islands, for example) likewise would be ruled out, and perhaps supersonic flight over main shipping routes also. Relatively few airports have runways long enough for SST take-off (two miles, plus extra for emergency) and few airports could tolerate the unbearably loud sideline noise the SSTs would make on taking off and landing.

Consider now questions of *finance*. Who will provide the billions of dollars required for start of mass production of the SSTs? If industry is unwilling to put up the $1 billion required for the present phase of the program, is it likely to muster the $4 to $8 billion needed for the later phases? (These are large numbers.

The entire cost of the World War II atomic bomb project was only $2 billion.)

Consider *purchase*. How many SSTs will actually be purchased? The price, $52 million and perhaps $60 to $80 million, is as great as the cost of building a first rate college or medical center. Few airlines could scrape up enough money to buy *one* such plane without borrowing from Wall Street. (What kind of SST service will an airline provide if it owns only, say, four SSTs? What happens when one of the four has mechanical or electrical trouble and is out of service for a week?) Which Wall Street financing institution will want to lend hundreds of millions of dollars to airlines that today are flying with 48 percent of the seats empty, are engaging in cut-throat competition, and at best barely manage to keep out of the red?

What about the foreign airlines that, it is claimed, would buy hundreds of the Boeing SSTs? Where would they obtain the billions of dollars needed?

Let us now take up *balance of payments*. If many Boeing SSTs are sold to foreign airlines, will this really help the U.S. balance of payments? A resounding *No* is given by the financial experts on the President's *SST ad hoc Review Committee* (see Appendix 4 for a verbatim account of their views). The large sum of money paid by those foreign airlines for the purchase of the Boeing SSTs would be more than offset by the *even larger* sums paid *to those airlines* by U.S. tourists (for airplane tickets to Europe, say) and by the additional billions of dollars those tourists would spend abroad for hotel rooms, food, and luxury purchases. Even the advocates of SSTs agree that sales of Boeing SSTs would be disappointingly small unless the speed of the SST stimulates millions more people to travel. Who will these people be, that travel in extra-fare planes? U.S. citizens, mainly. Thus the more SSTs are sold to foreign airlines, the more our balance of payments will be hurt—by U.S. citizens' buying flight tickets from the foreign airlines and making purchases abroad.

Pro-SST persons reply to this by saying: "But the Anglo-French Concorde SSTs will be flying then. Isn't it better to have the tourists fly in a Boeing SST than in a foreign SST?" There are two answers to this. First, there is excellent prospect that the Anglo-French Concorde project will be dropped. The plane has basically poor economics, there are no firm orders for it (and only 74 positions), and its price has escalated to more than $20,000,000. The take-off and landing noise would be intolerable at many major airports and its sonic boom would be intolerable over land, over islands, and perhaps over main shipping routes. The British Cabinet has already stated that the project may be reexamined or dropped if costs increase by 15 percent more (the costs are already about four times the original estimate). Second, the Boeing SST is not expected by its proponents to *replace* the Concorde but to supplement it—that is, to result in sales of many hundred *addition* ̄STs. This would result in an even greater outflow of U.S. dollars as the increasing numbers of our citizens flocked to foreign countires and spent large sums there.

Consider the little detail of *insurance*. Who would insure the SSTs? If a fully loaded SST were to crash, the damage claims for loss of passengers' lives could reach $50 million, and the loss of the plane itself would represent an additional $50 million. What insurance firm wants to gamble $100 million on a plane that admittedly contains dozens of radically new engineering features, requires two miles of runway, takes off at 220 mph, and is especially vulnerable to clear air turbulence, hail, lightning, and sabotage?

Now consider *creation of jobs*. SST proponents claim that the Boeing SST program would create 50,000 jobs directly and 150,000 jobs indirectly, and this would be a great benefit to the country (G-1). But experts on the *SST ad hoc Review Committee* dispose of this claim by pointing out that the more Boeing SSTs are built, the fewer subsonic planes would be built; in creating jobs building SSTs, we would be destroying jobs building jumbo jets and air busses. Also, the jobs created would be "concentrated in professional, managerial, skilled, and semi-skilled occupations which in a period of full employment, when these skills are in short supply, may prove inflationary. Very few unskilled workers will be required" (P-4, p. H-10434).

Creating jobs is never a problem. The *Wall Street Journal* pointed out on February 9, 1967, that creating new jobs is a poor excuse for embarking on a vast new project: "By that reasoning we should go around breaking windows so somebody could have the job of replacing them." The problem is to create jobs that result in real benefit to the country and give employment to persons who badly need work. The SST project fails on both counts. (Cannot any reader think of a hundred projects more deserving of support than an extra-fare airplane that could not be allowed to fly at cruising speed over land?)

Finally, there is the emotional question of *prestige*. Would we not suffer serious loss of prestige if we allowed some other country to build a faster plane than we produce? Could we abide seeing our President forced to travel in a foreign-built plane? The *SST ad hoc Review Committee* has answered these arguments by saying, in substance: if the British and French wish to build an uneconomic plane, let them! Let them be the ones to find that SSTs are expensive, dangerous, and unnecessary. Let them be the ones to reap the harvest of protests over take-off noise and sonic boom. Our aviation industry is second to none. We do not have to apologize for declining to pour billions of dollars into a doomed project—a multi-billion dollar *boomdoggle*.

Conclusion

The author's main concern is the SST's sonic boom—and the Federal Aviation Administration's refusal to establish a *definite* ban on supersonic flight overland. If overland supersonic flight is permitted, 500,000,000 persons in America, Europe, and Asia may be jolted every hour, day and night, by sonic booms from hit-and-run SSTs. People working, relaxing, sleeping will be banged repeatedly, without apology. Surgeons performing delicate operations will be startled, and their instinctive reflex reactions may cause permanent harm to the patients. The very elderly, the very young, and the ill will suffer more than other persons. Homes, hospitals, schools, and churches will no longer be havens from the bustle of modern life. In the U.S.A. alone the damage done to glass, plaster, and other materials may amount to $3,000,000 per day. For the aviation industry to make just and prompt payment for the damage done to buildings is impractical, and for it to make adequate payment for the harassment to people is inconceivable. Aviation, instead of being man's servant, would be his scourge.

Why should the public (95 or 98 percent of whose members would never fly in an SST) be forced to provide billions of dollars for an inefficient, unnecessary plane that could destroy peace and quiet throughout much of the civilized world?

Appendix I

Anti-Boom Groups

The following organizations are opposed to the sonic boom of the SST or have at least given very serious consideration to the threat of the sonic boom.

American Speech and Hearing Association, 9030 Old Georgetown Road, Washington, D.C., 20014. It sponsored the June 14, 1968 National Conference on Noise as a Public Health Hazard, at which many speakers warned of the threat of the sonic boom. See *Proceedings* dated February 1969 (A-3).

Anti-Concorde Project, 70 Lytton Avenue, Letchworth, Herts, England. Richard Wiggs, Convener. Issues newsletters and reports on sonic boom damage. Ran full-page advertisements in the *Times* and *Guardian*. Most active European anti-SST group.

Association Nationale contre Les Bangs Supersoniques, 94 Boulevard Flandrin, Paris 16e, France.

Citizens League Against the Sonic Boom, 19 Appleton Street, Cambridge, Massachusetts, 02138. Dr. William A. Shurcliff, Director. Dr. J. T. Edsall, Deputy Director. Membership: 3,500. Founded March 9, 1967. Issues fact-sheets, newsletters and "SST and Sonic Boom Handbook."

Comité Lyonnais contre le Bruit, Lyons, France. Prof. P. Mounier-Kuhn, President.

Conservation Foundation, 1250 Connecticut Avenue, N.W., Washington, D.C., 20036.

Eidgenössisches Aktionskomitee gegen den Uberschallknall ziviler Luftfahrzeuge, Schlossbergstrasse 22, Zollikon 8702, Switzerland. President: Dr. Meinrad Schär. Secretary: Dr. Andreas M. Rickenbach. Hopes to achieve, by popular vote, an amendment (to the constitution) which would ban supersonic flight by commercial aircraft over Switzerland.

Environmental Defense Fund, Inc., Post Office Building, Stony Brook, New York, New York, 11790.

Federation of Western Outdoor Clubs, 810½ Hampshire Street, San Francisco, California, 94110.

Freeman, Mrs. Arthur P., 3802 47 Street N.E., Seattle, Washington, 98105. Organized an anti-airport-noise and anti-boom group in Washington.

Friends of the Earth, 451 Pacific Avenue, San Francisco, California, 94133. David Brower, President.

International Congress for Noise Abatement (Association Internationale contre le Bruit), Zurich, Switzerland. At its fifth annual meeting (London, May 18, 1968) it passed a resolution calling on all governments to ban supersonic flights by SSTs.

Lundberg, B., former Director General of the Aeronautical Research Institute of Sweden. Holbergsgatan 120, 161/57 Bromma, Sweden. Most competent and persevering critic of the SST and its sonic boom.

National Academy of Sciences, Committee on SST-Sonic Boom, 2101 Constitution Avenue, N.W., Washington, D.C. Dr. John R. Dunning, Chairman of Committee. Reports and special releases have indicated that no avenue for large reduction in sonic boom is known and the present generation of SSTs will have considerably too intense a boom to be tolerated by people (N-1, N-2, N-3, N-4, B-2).

National Organization to Insure a Sound-Controlled Environment (NOISE). Created in the fall of 1969 to oppose airport noise, sonic boom, etc.

Organization for Economic Cooperation and Development, Paris, France. Has published many reports on sonic boom damage and held several international conferences to consider the threat of the sonic boom.

Santa Barbara, California, City Council. First city to pass an ordinance against all sonic booms. Ordinance 3246 approved November 16, 1967. (H-2).

Schweizerische Liga gegen den Lärm, Sihlstrasse 17, 8001 Zurich, Switzerland.

Sierra Club, 1050 Mills Tower, San Francisco, California. Published several articles, and one formal resolution, against the SST's boom.

U.S. Department of the Interior, Committee on Sonic Boom (*Science* December 19, 1967).

Wilderness Society, 729 15th Street, N.W., Washington, D.C., 20005. At its October 5, 1967 meeting it expressed concern over the SST's sonic boom. Its Resolution 12 urges that the production of sonic booms over land by SSTs be banned (*Living Wilderness,* Autumn 1967).

Appendix 2

Other Countries' Attitudes Toward the Sonic Boom

Canada

Canada has banned sonic booms that would cause damage. On November 10, 1967, Honorable Paul T. Hellyer, Canadian Minister of Transport, wrote to Mr. E. Jervis Bloomfield of Ioco, British Columbia, that Section 515 of the Canadian Air Regulations provides that:

"No aircraft shall be flown in such a manner as to create a shockwave the effect of which is to create or is likely to create a hazard to other aircraft or to persons or property on the ground."

Referring to questions as to whether the U.S.A. has permission to fly SSTs over Canada at supersonic speed, he wrote:

". . . I can assure you that no formal approach has been made to the Government of Canada for such permission and I can assure you that no such permission would be given unless it were in the Canadian public interest to do so. In any case, all such flights would be subject to the Canadian Air Regulations including the section quoted above."

Newspapers and individuals in Nova Scotia, Canada, have expressed alarm at the sonic boom threat, since the shortest routes from many eastern U.S. cities to Europe pass directly over Nova Scotia. See, for example, the main headline (in red!) of the Halifax *Chronicle-Herald* of May 8, 1967.

Residents of Ottawa, Ontario, and Kelowna, British Columbia, have had first-hand experience with sonic boom disasters in which $250,000 to $500,000 damage was done in a few seconds. See Chapter 4.

France

French newspapers have given prominence to the 13 deaths of Frenchmen from sonic booms (see Chapter 5). A 1967 report by French sonic boom experts mentions ". . . new and alarming evidence about the problem of the Concorde's sonic boom." The experts said that the bang-zone will be at least 40 miles wide, and that if a pilot, on seeing a city far ahead, tried to turn so as not to boom the city, "he would find it was already too late" (Paris Bureau, *Baltimore News American,* December 8, 1967).

In a poll, 35 percent of the French citizens interrogated said they "definitely could not" tolerate 10 booms a day (B-9).

Great Britain

A brief series of sonic boom tests was conducted over London and Bristol in the summer of 1967, and damage payments aggregated about $10,000 (see Chapter 4). No official conclusion was reached, but the consensus of opinion expressed in the British press appears to be that the booms were *not* acceptable. The Anti-Concorde Project is very active (see Appendix 1).

Ireland

Preparations for limiting or banning sonic booms from SSTs were announced in mid-September 1968 by the Honorable Erskine Childers, Minister for Transport and Power. He declared that sonic booms could prove obnoxious and inimical to the tranquility of the Irish countryside (*Irish Times,* mid-September 1968). He said: "I am adamant that the tranquility of this country should not be upset by sonic booms and it is for this reason that I have decided to introduce legislation" (letter of October 15, 1968).

Sweden

Sweden was one of the first countries to institute regulations against sonic booms that would damage property or awaken sleeping persons (per personal communication from P. Ahlmark, Member of the Swedish Parliament and initiator of the present regulations).

Mr. H. Winberg, Director General of the Swedish Air Board, is very active. Mr. B. Lundberg, "father of all objections to the sonic boom," has represented the Swedish Government at many sonic boom conferences; his extensive series of analyses of sonic boom damage and annoyance are listed in the bibliography.

In 1967 the Swedish government declared that "civil supersonic flight over Sweden will be prohibited if the sonic boom causes regular sleep disturbance or damage to property" (L-16).

Switzerland

Switzerland has announced that sonic booms intense enough to be annoying to people will not be permitted. The people have been warned that supersonic flights over their country could do many kinds of damage, including triggering avalanches (*Tribune de Geneve*, December 20, 1967). Late in 1969 the opponents of sonic booms were preparing to try to achieve an amendment (to the constitution) that would ban supersonic flight by commercial aircraft over Switzerland. See Appendix 1.

West Germany

"May I inform you that the German Government has stated on several occasions, that flight of civil aircraft at supersonic speed will not be tolerated if the intensity of the boom cannot be reduced significantly below the levels presently observed. Large scale annoyance of the public or damage to property will not be accepted" (letter of July 2, 1968, by the German Minister of Commerce).

Other Countries

The Netherlands may impose a ban on SSTs' sonic booms, according to *Aviation Daily*, May 9, 1969.

Bermuda may require SSTs—when at supersonic speed —to keep 100 miles away (letter of May 6, 1969, by Chief Secretary of Bermuda).

Appendix 3

Misleading Statements by the Federal Aviation Administration

First Misleading Statement

On June 22, 1967, General J. C. Maxwell, Director of the Federal Aviation Administration's SST Project, wrote to Congressman William H. Bates of Massachusetts:

> "In conclusion, we would like to emphasize that the sonic boom is not an uncontrollable phenomenon."

Fact: The sonic boom, like gravity, is a fact of nature. Aerodynamics experts who have spent years doing research on the sonic boom admit that there simply is no way to eliminate the boom. Moreover, there is *no avenue even remotely in sight* whereby any great reduction can be made in the severity of the sonic boom to be produced by the proposed SSTs. Recent changes in designs of SSTs have actually *increased* the boom intensity.

Second Misleading Statement

In that same June 22, 1967, letter General Maxwell said:

> "The SST, for example, has excellent sonic boom characteristics for an aircraft of its size and weight."

Fact: The Boeing SST is to be the heaviest supersonic plane in existence and its boom is expected to be more intense than that from any other plane in existence flying at similar altitude and speed.

Third Misleading Statement

In a speech delivered on March 14, 1967, Mr. A. H. Skaggs, Chief of the FAA's SST Economics Section, declared (according to the FAA release):

> "It takes a boom of well over 5 pounds per square foot to do property damage, such as cracking plaster."

Fact: In the long and elaborate sonic boom tests conducted by the FAA over Oklahoma City in 1964, the average boom

111

overpressure (according to the official Government report) was only about 1.3 psf. Yet more than 4,000 claims for damage to window glass, plaster, etc., were filed by Oklahoma residents. The house of Mr. Bailey Smith, at 1804 NE 67 Street, was damaged so severely that a Federal circuit court awarded him $10,000. By mid-1969 the total damage awards to Oklahoma City homeowners amounted to over $123,000, and $128,000 in additional claims was still in litigation.

Fourth Misleading Statement

In countless statements and releases, FAA officials have stated that

"The development funds being advanced by the Government for the SST will be restored through royalty payments . . ." and "The financing arrangements provide for recoupment . . ."

Fact: There is no provision insuring restoration of funds to the Government, and no assurance of recoupment. There is a royalty-payment clause in the contract with Boeing Co., but the clause is so flexible that it could happen that Boeing could sell dozens of SSTs without paying any royalty at all; and if there were no further sales, the Government would not recover a penny. The Government would not recoup unless 300 SSTs were sold. (*Congressional Hearings,* U-5).

Fifth Misleading Statement

General J. C. Maxwell, when FAA Head of SST Development, wrote:

"There is no dependence on overland flight as necessary to the economic success of the SST. More than 70 percent of the world's airlanes lie over oceans . . ."

Fact: The 70 percent figure is a gross overstatement. Attempting to explain General Maxwell's statement, B. J. Vierling, Acting Head of SST Development, stated that (1) General Maxwell should have said "world's international airlanes," not "world's airlanes," and (2) that: "Substantiating the conclusions of the study is the well-known fact that water covers 70 percent of the earth's surface." This is no substantiation. *Water coverage* and *airline routes* are two very different subjects. If the Pacific Ocean covers

30 percent of the earth's surface, does this mean that 30 percent of the air routes are over the Pacific? Obviously not.

Appendix 4

Reports by the Four Working Panels of the President's SST ad hoc Review Committee

(Note: On October 31, 1969, the long-withheld report of March 1969 by the President's SST ad hoc Review Committee was released to the public: it was reprinted in the October 31 *Congressional Record* (pp. H-10432—H-10446) at the request of Congressman S. R. Yates (D., Ill.). The main content is the set of four reports by the Committee's working panels. These four reports are presented here in full. A summary prepared by the Department of Transportation staff is not included here, since a majority of the Committee members issued statements declaring that the summary was biased and misrepresented the views of the panels. Some of these critical statements are appended.)

Introductory Remarks by Congressman S. R. Yates

Mr. YATES. Mr. Speaker, the Subcommittee on Appropriations, of which I am a member, recently completed its hearings on the Department of Transportation. Among the appropriations requests was one for the SST. It was at my request that there was included in the hearings the report of the SST ad hoc review committee which was stated to have been made available to President Nixon by the Department of Transportation before he announced his decision to continue with the SST program. That report was made public today.

The report of that committee is so unfavorable to the program that I am amazed that President Nixon approved the request for the SST. The committee, which consisted of many of the ablest people in this administration, recommended overwhelmingly in favor of suspending work on the project.

The report rejects basic arguments used to justify the SST. It disputes that the balance of payments would be favorable; it casts doubt on the economic viability of the plane; it questions whether Americans will ever accept the jarring sonic boom which is an inseparable part of supersonic flight, it raises disturbing questions about the damaging effects the SST would have on the environment, it criticizes the two-headed conflicting role played by the FAA in acting as the guardian of the safety of the Nation's airways and of the aircraft using the airways. While acting at the same time as the principal supporter and loving promoter of an aircraft having such dubious value as the SST.

Mr. Speaker, when President Kennedy launched the SST program in 1963 he said:

In no event will the Government investment be permitted to exceed $750 million.

With the appropriation proposed for this year expenditures on the project will very nearly reach the limit set by President Kennedy, and if the appropriations scheduled to be made over the next 5 years are added, this airplane will cost more than one-half billion dollars than the amount that Mr. Kennedy established. I believe this is the logical time to call a halt to the program and I shall try to strike the appropriation in my committee.

Creation of the Committee and Main Witnesses

THE WHITE HOUSE,
Washington, February 19, 1969.

Memorandum for Mr. James Beggs.

I am establishing an ad hoc committee to review the Supersonic Transport program in line with the recommendations given to me by Secretary Volpe.

I hereby appoint you the Chairman of this Committee. The other members of the committee will be:

Mr. Rocco Siciliano, Under Secretary of Commerce.

Dr. Robert C. Seamans, Jr., Secretary of the Air Force.

Mr. John Veneman, Under Secretary of HEW.

Mr. Russell Train, Under Secretary of the Interior.

Mr. Richard G. Kleindienst, Deputy Attorney General.

Mr. Arnold Weber, Assistant Secretary of Labor.

Ambassador U. Alexis Johnson, Under Secretary of State.

Mr. Paul Volcker, Under Secretary of the Treasury.

Dr. Henry Houthakker, Member, Council of Economic Advisers.

Dr. Lee A. DuBridge, National Science Adviser.

Mr. Charles W. Harper, Deputy Associate Administrator of NASA.

The activities of this committee should be coordinated closely with the Bureau of the Budget.

RICHARD NIXON.

WORKING PANEL COMPOSITION

(1) Balance of Payments and International Relations Panel Representatives from Treasury (Chairman), Commerce and State.

(2) Technological Fall-Out Panel—Representatives from the Office of Science and Technology (Chairman), Department of Defense, and NASA.

(3) Environmental and Sociological Impact Panel—Representatives from HEW (Chairman), Interior, and Office of Science and Technology.

(4) Economics Panel—Representatives from the Council of Economic Advisers (Chairman), Labor and Commerce.

WITNESSES WHO ADDRESSED THE COMMITTEE

Dr. Arnold Moore, Director, Naval Warfare Analysis Group, Center for Naval Analyses.

Mr. Gerald Kraft, President, Charles River Associates.

Mr. Najeeb Halaby, President, Pan American.

Mr. Robert Rummel, Vice President, TWA.

Mr. Harding Lawrence, President, Braniff.

Mr. Karl Harr, Jr., President, Aerospace Industries Association.

Prof. William A. Shurcliff, Director, Citizens League Against the Sonic Boom.

Lt. Gen. Elwood R. Quesada, Chairman of the Board and President, the L'Enfant Plaza Corps.

Report By Panel on Balance of Payments and International Relations

Potential Impact of an SST on the U.S.
Balance of Payments

Introduction of a supersonic aircraft will affect several closely interrelated components of the U.S. balance of payments:

Aircraft exports and imports (supersonic and subsonic):

U.S. travel abroad and foreign travel to the U.S.;

The distribution of this travel between U.S. and foreign airlines;

U.S. port expenditures by foreign airlines and port expenditures abroad by U.S. airlines;

The amount of export credit extended or received by the U.S. in connection with aircraft financing; and

General U.S. imports and exports, and U.S. investments abroad, all of which will be facilitated by the greater ease of U.S. business travel abroad due to the SST.

There are two widely divergent views about which of the above items should be considered in appraising the balance-of-payments impact of an SST. The first view is that only the aircraft account (and possibly port expenditures) should be considered. The basis for this view is that the U.S. has a long-run interest in encouraging the development and operation of better means of international transportation in the interests of the entire world economy; and that if a U.S. SST increases our aircraft exports (or decreases our aircraft imports) there is no U.S. balance-of-payments reason for not pursuing this long-run interest by production of a U.S. SST. The Commerce Department supports this view.

The second point of view is that all the above items must be considered, insofar as feasible, in appraising the balance-of-payments impact of an SST. The logic of this position is especially clear with respect to two of the above items: U.S. aircraft exports and U.S. travel abroad.

The amount of export contribution (a *plus* item) which a U.S. SST makes to the U.S. balance of payments depends in considerable part on the additional U.S. travel abroad (a *minus* item in our balance of payments) induced by the time savings on an SST. Since the *plus* item depends substantially on the *minus* item, both (as well as other relevant items) must be considered in appraising U.S. balance-of-payments impact.

State and Treasury support this second view.

In line with the above divergence of views, Section A of the attachment comments on the estimated impact of an SST only on the aircraft account in our balance of payments. The conclusion in this respect is:

If only the aircraft account is considered, there is no *balance-of-payments* reason for delaying the SST project, regardless of whether or not a commercially viable foreign supersonic aircraft emerges.

Section B of the attachment comments on the effects on other balance-of-payments items, primarily the U.S. travel deficit. The conclusion is:

If the U.S. over-all balance of payments is considered, there is substantial reason for delay in proceeding to the next stage of the SST project—prototype production. The reason lies in the large adverse effect on the U.S. travel deficit of a U.S. SST in the absence of a commercially viable Concorde *plus* doubt about the Concorde's becoming a commercially viable plane.

Results of the Concorde prototype testing over the next 12 months will throw further light on its chances of becoming commercially viable. The U.S., in addition to continuing further research in aircraft and engine design, could profitably use this period to update and improve the surveys of the effect of supersonic transportation on both the aircraft and travel accounts. The assumptions currently being used for dividing traffic between supersonic and subsonic aircraft and for estimating additional speed-induced travel are critical to both the aircraft and travel accounts and are subject to a high margin of error.

(A) *SST Impact on Aircraft Account in the U.S. Balance of Payments:* If there is a commercially viable *foreign* supersonic aircraft in existence, a competitive U.S. SST would improve the *aircraft account* in the U.S. balance of payments by reducing U.S. imports of the foreign supersonic; resulting in U.S. supersonic exports of greater value than the subsonic exports which are displaced.

There is a wide range of benefit estimates based on different assumptions about fares, passenger evaluation of time savings, etc. Also, benefits vary depending on the assumed market situations.

On a current cash basis, the FAA analysis indicates a total improvement of about $17 billion over the period through 1990, from introducing a U.S. SST in 1978 into competition with a Concorde.

If there is no commercially viable Concorde, the improvement in the aircraft account through 1990 due to a U.S. SST (beginning operations in 1978) is estimated at $11 billion—that is, an increase from around $17 billion of subsonic exports in the absence of *any* supersonic plane to $28 billion of combined SST and subsonic exports.

(B) *SST Impact on Various Accounts in the U.S. Balance of Payments:* U.S. aircraft sales and U.S. travel expenditures abroad have divergent effects on the balance of payments.

While an increase in exports of SST's will benefit the aircraft account, it will produce an even larger increase in the travel deficit, as long as Americans make the majority of supersonic trips.

The current rate of air travel deficit—including aircraft port expenditures, travelers' fares and travelers' expenditures in foreign countries, is approximately $1.6 billion. *Even in the absence of any commercial supersonic aircraft,* it is expected to increase in absolute amount, although at a reduced rate of increase, over the next few decades, totaling around $70 billion for the period 1971 through 1990—the period used by the consultant firm which has made the only quantitative analysis of the potential impact of the supersonic transportation on several relevant items in the balance of payments.

That analysis (performed in 1966) produced an unrealistically high estimate of the adverse impact on the U.S. travel account of speed-induced supersonic travel in the 20-year period. It would make the $70 billion figure mentioned above over twice as large. Use of a longer base period for determining statistical relationships, a re-examination of some of the underlying assumptions, and use of more realistic in-service dates for supersonic aircraft are believed likely to reduce the 1966 estimate substantially.

Even a more conservative estimate from revised underly assumptions is likely to indicate an adverse impact of speed-induced supersonic travel on the U.S. travel account considerably greater than the estimated *beneficial* impact of supersonic aircraft sales on the U.S. aircraft account.

The latter judgment depends heavily on whether or not a *commercially viable* foreign supersonic aircraft is assumed to be in operation when a U.S. SST is put in service. If such a foreign aircraft is assumed not to be in operation, the entire adverse travel impact of speed-induced supersonic travel must be attributed to the U.S. SST.

At present the commercial viability of the Concorde is very much in doubt—particularly because of landing and take-off noise, range limitations and prospective high operating cost per seat mile. Cables from our embassies in London and Paris indicate that some French and British officials close to the program are skeptical of the Concorde's commercial viability.

Foreign Relations Impact of U.S. SST Decision

The Anglo-French Concorde program has been a sensitive domestic issue in those countries, particularly the U.K. U.S. actions on the SST question which seem to the U.K. and France as designed to scuttle the Concorde for competitive reasons will undoubtedly stimulate an adverse political reaction. On the other hand, a U.S. decision to proceed in an orderly fashion, to delay, or to abandon the U.S. program on sensible technical and economic grounds should not generate an adverse Anglo-French reaction.

A more difficult question is raised by the problem of airport noise generated by SST's. U.S. noise standards could conceivably bar the Concorde from access to the principal U.S. international airports which would undoubtedly doom the Concorde program. It is therefore imperative that we keep the British and French advised of U.S. noise developments to insure their full understanding, if not acceptance, of the U.S. position on noise. In this connection, it would be desirable for the United States to seek early international agreement on noise standards, including airport noise created by SST's.

Report By Panel on Economics

The Economic Subcommittee is struck by the large amount of uncertainty connected with the SST program. Almost every economic aspect of the program reflects unverifiable matters of judgment with great variance in the opinion of experts. Probably the single most uncertain aspect of the whole program relates to the uncertainty as to whether an SST can be built in the given time that will meet the specifications of being efficient, safe, and economical.

The record to date is not completely reassuring. After extensive study, the previous design was accepted as a good design that would produce an SST with the desired characteristics, but failed. While we are assured that the current design will succeed, the previous committee was given similar assurance. Assuming the prototype design meets its objectives, major innovations will still have to be made to produce an economical SST. Past commercial plane developments have never involved such a large jump in technology. In the case of commercial transports, a new type of metal—titanium—must be fabricated; a new type of guidance and electric control system must be developed; more efficient and quieter engines must be produced.

No doubt, all of the technical problems are eventually solvable, but how soon and at what cost? The record for new aircraft being designed to make technological jumps of this magnitude is confined strictly to military production. The record in those cases in not good. Production costs have often been more than three times what they were predicted to be. The record of civilian production of new planes has undoubtedly been much better. Most civilian jet transports have met their design goals with respect to performance and price and their performance has been improved during the economic life of the plane. However, these aircraft were designed from well known technology. For example, the 707 was a commercial adaption of an already developed and well tested Air Force plane. The developmental experience with the Concorde gives little cause for optimism; developmental costs have more than doubled.

These comments do not mean that we believe that the plane cannot be built to meet the specifications at the forecasted costs but simply that there is a large element of doubt. If the forecasts turn out to be incorrect, costs could escalate considerably.

Demand

Estimating future demand involves another area of considerable certainty. Each element in the IDA model for forecasting demand involves large uncertainties and considerable elements of judgment in which reasonable people may come to considerably different opinions. Total demand for the SST will depend on total revenue passenger miles in the future. The IDA model basically forecasts the growth rate at approximately 10 percent per year. Historical experience, especially the last few years, suggests that a higher rate would be more accurate. However, it should be noted that IDA forecast a higher rate in the near future and a lower rate in the more distant future.

Revenue passenger miles in 1968 were 30 percent above IDA's forecast. If we extend IDA's rate of growth from that base level, total revenue passenger miles in 1969 will be 30 percent higher than forecast with an increase of approximately 150 aircraft. However, airport congestion which has already reached serious proportions in international terminals such as Kennedy, may prevent this traffic growth from being achieved.

The market for supersonic transport will depend on the supersonic-subsonic split. This depends in turn on those markets which are open to supersonic flight, on the relative fare between supersonic and subsonic, and on how the public values time saved. The FAA has assumed that the public will pay one and a half times their hourly earnings to secure an hour's reduction in flight time. IDA, after having looked at some very sketchy evidence, concluded that the travellers value their time at their hourly earning rate. A 1967 Ph. D. study done by Ruben Gronau at Columbia University under the direction of Gary Becker concluded on the basis of a very detailed statistical study of air travel time from New York City to other points that businessmen value their time in air travel at 0.4 times their average hourly family income and that pleasure travellers valued their time in aircraft travel at zero. On the other hand, earlier estimates by the airlines indicate value of time from 1.3 to 2.1 times earnings.

The effect of assuming different values of time is substantial. Under the base case for the FAA with consumers valuing their time at one and a half times their hourly earnings, 500 planes will be sold. If, on the other hand, IDA is correct and they value time at one times their hourly earnings, only 350 planes will be sold.

In summary, the great uncertainties relating to estimating the public's valuation of time leaves the projected market subject to wide error.

Whatever the value of time, the split between supersonic and subsonic would depend upon the relative fares. If supersonic fares equal subsonic, all or almost all will travel by supersonic. The FAA in their base case has assumed that supersonic will have a 25 percent premium over the subsonic. The airlines are hoping for something less. The FAA predicated their relative fare position on the basis that the American SST seat costs would be roughly equal to the subsonic fares existing in 1965. They assumed that subsonic fares between 1965 and 1978 would decline in real terms by about 25 percent, producing the 25 percent differential. However, between 1965 and 1968 subsonic fares have already declined 18 percent. If one assumes as did IDA and the FAA that fares decline by 1.8 percent per year in the future, by 1978 the relative difference in supersonic and subsonic fares will grow to 36 percent rather than 25 percent. Such an increase in the difference between fares will reduce plane sales by about 150. However, airlines may be willing to accept a lower rate of return in order to preserve a 25 percent fare differential, with the result that the same 500 planes will be sold.

These plane fares, however, are highly speculative. They, of course, depend on the price of the plane and its operating costs which as has been pointed out above are highly uncertain. Both IDA and the FAA feasibility study assumed that the Concorde would not compete in the same markets with SST. Since the Concorde will be introduced five years prior to the SST, it may secure a considerable market before the SST is introduced. While the SST is expected to have operating costs below those of the Concorde, it may not be able to secure lower fares.

International fares are set by unanimous agreement of IATA in which each airline has a vote. With many airlines having the Concorde and with two airlines being intimately connected with its production—BOAC and Air France—it seems unlikely that the SST will force supersonic fares below those that are economical for the Concorde and drive the Concorde out of the market—the FAA assumption. The Concorde will be sold for about half the price and will have the seating capacity of an SST. Thus, two Concordes can be secured for each SST giving airlines an additional flexibility in scheduling. If fares are kept high enough to protect the Concorde so that both types of supersonic planes operate in the same markets at the same price, then they may split the market which will reduce SST sales from 500 to 250.

Another imponderable in the market forecast involves restrictions that might be imposed because of noise. The supersonic planes are by general agreement very noisy. Whether the planes will be permitted to land at major airports is uncertain. How much noise will the public tolerate? Problems clearly exist for Miami International, Boston's

Logan Airport, and Los Angeles Airport. However, the planned or proposed construction of new airports may alleviate the problem. It is not clear how much of the added costs of new airports would be attributable to supersonic transports.

It should be noted that by the terms of the FAA-Boeing contract, Boeing establishes the price of the plane. Given the demand model specified, Boeing . . . could make more money at a price of $40 million than at a price of $37 million. In fact, Boeing could maximize its profits if it charged about $48 million. Such a price would reduce sales of planes to something under 350. This would in turn reduce government royalties to the point that the government barely got its money back.

Financing

Will the operation of the proposed U.S. SST provide a sufficient rate of return to the airlines to insure purchase of 500 U.S. SST's?

Since the SST is more capital intensive than subsonic aircraft, it is more sensitive to lower earnings. The model assumes that the higher rate of return earned on long-haul operations in the past will continue during the SST period.

The predicted ROI for the airline depends on the airlines achieving a load factor of 58 percent. This is relatively high compared to the experience of U.S. international and territorial airlines during the last two years or even the average for the seven years.

If load factors were to continue at the 1968 level of 52.6 percent throughout the SST period, 1978–1990, the return of investment to the airlines would only be 22.2 percent of the aircraft sales price compared to a ROI of 28.3 for the base case.

Statistics for the past seven years indicate that a lower overall load factor than 58 percent should probably be used in evaluating the SST program since this rate was achieved only once (1969) in the past seven years. The 1962–68 average of 55 percent would yield an airline ROI of 25.2 percent before taxes.

Moreover, long haul rates of return have been declining and were about 10.5 percent in 1968. Whether lower rates of return are practical is clearly uncertain. The problem of financing such a huge investment on top of the large investment in jumbo jets could ?????? Copy missing

Financing the manufacture and purchases of the SST could prove more difficult than anticipated. It is generally accepted that the engine manufacturer will have the capacity to generate the necessary financing required. However, the EFR expresses some doubts regarding the airframe manufacturer: "Pending receipt of the financial plan from the airframe manufacturer, a reasonable approach suggests that any program decisions consider the possibility that the Government may be required to act as a guarantor of or to provide any additional funds needed by the airframe manufacturer."

Requirements
[In millions]

Facilities	$278
Development costs	1,226
Leadtime production costs	1,295
Total	3,429

Source of funds
[In millions]

Government prototype participation	$726
Airline prepayments	1,348
Tax considerations	310
Manufacturers shortage	1,045
Total	3,429

"This situation is expected to continue through 1975 at which point a cumulative financing of $1,064 million will exist . . . well in excess of twice the Boeing Company's net worth as of December 31, 1965."

Recent comments in the trade press indicate that the financing problem is more acute today due to increased costs and Boeing's additional developmental expenditures. The 747, 767, and SST programs could strain Boeing's financial and managerial resources. If the SST program is approved, Boeing might have to cut back some of its subsonic 767, 747, 727, or 707 activities.

The EFR assumed that the U.S. airline industry could provide 86 percent of its total cash requirements for the large subsonic and Concorde equipment cycle (1967–74)

from internal cash generation (net income, depreciation, and disposal of flight equipment) and provide about 80 percent of its requirements for the heavy SST start-up costs during 1975-77 from the same sources.

The recent decline in rates of return on investment (8.9% in 1966, 7.7% in 1967, and an estimated 6% for 1968) suggests that the airline industry may already be overcapitalized. Declining earnings ratios will make it more difficult to obtain the large sums required for SST's from internal sources and require more expensive commercial financing.

Employment

Under the FAA base case the SST program may generate total employment, both direct and indirect, in excess of 100,000 workers, an unknown proportion of which will result from relative declines in other parts of the aerospace industry. This employment will be highly concentrated in professional, managerial, skilled, and semi-skilled occupations which in a period of full employment, when these skills are in short supply, may prove inflationary. Very few unskilled workers will be required. However, such employment should not be considered as a justification for proceeding with the program but only as a dividend from it.

Report By Panel on Environmental and Sociological Impact

REPORT OF THE ENVIRONMENTAL AND SOCIOLOGICAL PANEL OF THE AD HOC SUPERSONIC TRANSPORT REVIEW COMMITTEE

Introduction

Supersonic transport (SST) has the potential for intensifying hazards to the passengers and crew for causing significant further deterioration in the environment for people on the ground particularly in the vicinity of SST airports and along SST flight paths. In recognition of their respective responsibilities in this regard in 1968, the Department of Health, Education, and Welfare established a "Committee on Health Effects of Supersonic Transport," and the Department of the Interior assembled a "Special Study Group on Noise and Sonic Boom in Relation to Man." The Committee on Environmental Quality of the Federal Council for Science and Technology in July 1967 established a Task Force to report on noise as an environmental problem.

The Panel has drawn freely on the findings of each of

these committees and has also been guided by the SST reports and briefings provided by the Department of Transportation.

The object of this report is to identify significant potential environmental and sociological problems related to the health and well-being of people which must be considered in making decisions concerning the SST. Technological, economic and political factors both domestic and international traditionally considered in developing national policy with respect to such matters are insufficient with respect to the SST.

The Panel considers the principal environmental and sociological problem areas to be: (1) Sonic boom; (2) Airport noise; (3) Hazards to passengers and crew; and (4) Effects of water vapor in the stratosphere.

Sonic boom

All available information indicates that the effects of sonic boom are such as to be considered intolerable by a very high percentage of the people affected. The Panel is cognizant of statements and reports to the effect that supersonic flight over U.S. continental land areas is not contemplated at this time and that SST design and development is proceeding on this assumption. However, the Panel is very concerned about the economic pressures that will be exerted if it is subsequently found that the economic success of the aircraft depends on overland flights at supersonic speeds. For this reason the Panel believes it is essential that the public be formally assured by appropriate authorities that commercial supersonic flights over land will not be permitted and that SST design, development, and economic considerations are and will remain restricted to over water routes.

Airport noise

The rapid growth of the air transportation system has resulted in a wave of public reaction to aircraft noise on and near major airports and many smaller ones around the world. The problem can be characterized as one of conflict between two groups—those who benefit from air transportation services and people who live and work in communities near airports. The conflict exists because social and economic costs resulting from aircraft noise are imposed upon certain land users in the vicinity of airports who receive no direct benefits.

"The development of methods to reduce engine noise is an essential element in the development of the SST as well as subsonic jet aircraft. Reduction of engine noise, however, is more difficult for the SST. Acceleration to supersonic speeds and efficient supersonic cruise require engines with high-temperature high-velocity jets. These engines are fundamentally noisier than the fan engines that are optimum for the subsonic jets." (The SST Program and Related National

Benefits Feb. 17, 1969, the Boeing Company, page 6–22.)

According to estimates provided by the FAA, the levels of noise over a community on takeoff directly under the flight path one mile beyond a 10,000 foot runway, with power reduced to hold a rate of climb of 500 feet per minute, are 111 PNdB (perceived noise in decibels) for the SST and 125 PNdB for the 707. On final approach one mile out from the runway the level for the SST is 109 PNdB and for the 707, 123 PNdB. For the SST the 100 PNdB contour extends laterally 6000 feet on either side of the runway when the plane is 200 feet in the air at the end of the runway on takeoff. The comparative 100 PNdB contour for the 707 is about 2000 feet on either side of the runway. At the three mile point on takeoff, the 100 PNdB contour extends about 2000 feet on either side of the flight line for both the SST and the 707. By way of comparison, a trailer truck at highway speed has an over-all sound level of about 90 dB at 20 feet, a pavement breaker about 115 dB at the operator's ear, and the values of 109 and 111 PNdB cited above for the SST are in the range of PNdB levels recorded indoors and outdoors during sonic booms from B-58 aircraft. On the ground the SST is significantly noisier than the 707, the 100 PNdB contour extending about 5000 feet in all directions at the starting point and from 5000 to 6000 feet on either side of the runway during takeoff roll. The data indicate that on landing and takeoff the SST can be expected to produce noise levels exceeding 100 PNdB over a distance of 13 miles. An area 4 miles long and approximately 2 miles wide surrounding the runway would be exposed to noise levels in excess of 100 PNdB.

Prolonged exposure to intense noise produces permanent hearing loss. Increasing numbers of competent investigators believe that such exposure may adversely affect other organic, sensory and physiologic functions of the human body. Noise may also disrupt job performance by interfering with speech communication, distracting attention, and otherwise complicating the demands of the task. Such disruption could cause losses in overall efficiency or require increased effort and concentration to cope with the work situation. With regard to the latter, there appears to be a close relationship between bodily fatigue and noise exposure. Noise-induced hearing loss looms as a major health hazard in American industry. However, despite numerous efforts by professional standards and criteria committees, a national hearing conservation standard governing allowable or safe exposures remains to be established. Aside from hearing loss, noise may cause cardiovascular, glandular, respiratory, and neurologic changes, all of which are suggestive of a general stress reaction. Whether such reactions have pathologic consequences is not really known. However, there are growing indications, mainly in the foreign scientific literature, that routine exposures to intense industrial noise may lead to chronic physiologic disturbances. Available information suggests that workers devoting constant attention to detail (e.g., quality inspection, console monitoring) may be most prone to distraction. Noise may mask auditory warning signals and thereby cause accidents or generate reactions of annoyance and general fatigue.

Although some reduction in SST engine noise may be expected to result from expanded research and development programs on engine design and flight operating procedures, information available at this time indicates that land use planning in the vicinity of airports is the only satisfactory solution to this problem.

On the basis of the information summarized above, the panel is of the opinion that noise levels associated with SST operations will exceed 100 PNdB over large areas surrounding SST airports. It can be expected, therefore, that significant numbers of people will file complaints and resort to legal action, and that a very high percentage of the exposed population will find the noise intolerable and the apparent cause of a wide variety of adverse effects.

Hazards to passengers and crew

There is an urgent need to carefully evaluate the inherent operational and environmental hazards that will be encountered while accelerating from zero to Mach 3 and cruising at supersonic speeds in a hostile environment. Passengers and crew will be vulnerable to a number of potentially serious physical, physiological, and psychological stresses associated with rapid acceleration, gravitational changes, reduced barometric pressure, increased ionizing radiation, temperature changes, and aircraft noise and vibration.

Man cannot tolerate acceleration loads above 4 to 5 g. Visual disturbances occur between 3 and 4 g. At 5 g. loss of consciousness occurs. Turbulent flight may cause brief linear acceleration of 10 to 12 g. which could cause fractures in unrestrained persons. Angular accelerations in turns and linear-angular accelerations during turbulent flight are important causes of motion sickness. Under cruise conditions the SST's exterior skin temperature will approach 260° C. Therefore, it is necessary to insulate the cabin and to install refrigeration, whereas subsonic jets require heating at cruise altitudes because the external temperature is approximately 55 degrees below zero centigrade.

Ozone is present in a concentration of about 8 ppm at 65,000 feet. There is ample evidence that ozone is a highly toxic substance which must not be allowed to enter the plane. A doubling of the present flight altitude reduces ambient air pressure from one-fifth to one-thirtieth that at sea level. Therefore, in order to maintain current cabin pressures equivalent to an altitude of 7,500 feet, pressurization of the SST must be increased by approximately 2.5 psi above subsonic jets. A loss of pressure at 65,000 feet would result in all aboard losing consciousness within fifteen seconds.

The radiation hazard would be approximately 100 times greater than at ground level. A flight crew exposed for 600 hours annually will accumulate 0.85 rem (roentgen-equivalent-man) from this source alone. When this value is compared with the Maximum Permissible Dose of 0.5 rem for the general public, the question arises whether SST crews should be placed in the category of radiation workers and kept under close surveillance. The advisability of allowing pregnant women, especially in the first trimester, to travel in these planes, and of limiting diagnostic x-rays for individuals who fly SST's will also need to be considered. Much higher rates of exposure associated with solar flares are to be avoided by utilizing a warning network which will permit the pilot to descend to safer altitudes. Criteria should be developed to guide prospective passengers afflicted with chronic diseases for whom the environmental stresses which might conceivably be encountered could be detrimental to their health. Lastly, special consideration should be given to the bio-instrumentation of flight crews in view of experiences in manned space flight which have demonstrated the occurrence of serious loss of insight and judgment which accompany stress such as hypoxia or fatigue. At the earliest indication of malfunction of the aircraft, especially in its pressurization, temperature control, or oxygen systems, the aircraft must be brought down to safe levels as quickly as possible either by the crew or by the automatic pilot. The health and welfare of crews and passengers are incomparably more dependent on the proper functioning of equipment for the SST than for subsonic aircraft.

Effects of water vapor in the stratosphere

The widespread use of supersonic transports will introduce large quantities of water vapor into the stratosphere. The weight of water vapor released is about 40% greater than the weight of the fuel consumed. Four hundred SST's flying four trips per day might release an amount of water vapor per day that is 0.025% of that naturally present in the altitude range in which the flights occur. The introduction of this additional water vapor into the stratosphere can produce two effects which may be important:

(1) Persistent contrails might form to such an extent that there would be a significant increase in cirrus clouds;

(2) There could be a significant increase in the relative humidity of the stratosphere even if there were no significant increase in the extent of cirrus cloudiness.

Both effects would alter the radiation balance and thereby possibly affect the general circulation of atmospheric components. Of greater significance may be the local contamination one can expect from a high concentration of flights over the North Atlantic. If half the activity is concentrated over 5% of the earth's surface, local contamination would be ten times larger than calculated above on a global basis or about 0.25% per day of the naturally present water vapor. However, the local concentration of water vapor from flights on crowded routes may spread out rapidly and be of no real significance.

Although it would appear that geophysical effects are probably minor, they certainly should not be neglected. Data required include information relevant to the horizontal mixing times within the stratosphere and to the resident time of gases within the stratosphere. With these parameters at hand, it should be possible to construct a numerical model of the stratosphere to determine more accurately the possible radiative effects on the general circulation.

The findings of the Committees referred to in the Introduction are contained in the following reports, copies of which have been provided to the Ad Hoc SST Review Committee Staff:

1. "Noise—Sound Without Value," Committee on Environmental Quality of the Federal Council for Science and Technology, September 1968.

2. "Report to the Secretary of the Interior of the Special Study Group on Noise and Sonic Boom in Relation to Man"

3. "Supersonic Transport (SST)—Potential Health Hazards to the Crew, Passengers, and Population" (Unpublished Draft) Consumer Protection and Environmental Health Service, DHEW.

Report By Panel on Technological Fallout

PURPOSE

To examine the importance of the SST program to the overall national research and development posture, the technological fallout benefits that may result from the SST program and specifically whether such benefits have security value.

SUMMARY CONCLUSION

The SST program will advance many areas of technology and will result in technological fallout both to the aircraft industry in general and to other industrial and military applications. The magnitude of this effect is very difficult to assess, but it appears to be small. Nevertheless, there are a number of areas which can be identified as having a high probability of potential benefit, such as: flight control systems, structures, materials, aircraft engines, aerodynamics.

While technological fallout will inevitably result from a complex, high technology program such as the SST development, the value of this benefit appears to be limited. We believe technological fallout to be of relatively minor importance in this program and therefore should not be considered either wholly or in part as a basis for justifying the program. In the SST program, fallout or technological advancement should be considered as a bonus or additional benefit from a program which must depend upon other reasons for its continuation.

These views are developed in greater detail in the sections which follow.

APPROACH

In order to develop a report responsive to the tasks outlined above, the following questions were considered.

1. What are the principal areas of technology which will be advanced by the SST prototype program?

2. What value or importance do these technologies have to our national research and development posture?

3. What are the national security implications of technologies advanced by the SST program? Are they unique to the SST or will other programs provide similar benefits?

We shall discuss each in turn.

Question 1: What are the principal areas of technology which will be advanced by the SST prototype program?

Aircraft technology will be advanced in a number of areas and this will enhance future development of both military and civil aircraft. There are aspects of this technology which will not only be beneficial to future aircraft development but should have more general application as well.

Aircraft Technology

1. *Aerodynamics*—The SST will require high aerodynamic efficiency over its complete speed range. Achievement

of high levels of performance will provide useful correlation between theory and experiment, and extensive experience of use in the design of future aircraft.

2. *Advanced Flight Controls*—The SST demands on airplane empty weight will assist in achieving advances in flight control systems which are being considered for other advanced subsonic aircraft. These advanced systems include: (a) fly-by-wire techniques which result in lower system weight than the conventional cable-pulley-hydraulic system. (b) Stability augmentation systems resulting in saving of aircraft weight through use of smaller control surfaces. (c) Control systems for suppression of flutter loading resulting in additional savings in aircraft structural weight.

3. *Aircraft Tires*—In order to meet airline operational requirements, an improvement in aircraft tires is required for the SST. The improvement expected will enhance tire life in general and will be applicable broadly to other aircraft.

4. *High Temperature Structures*—The design of structures that operate at elevated temperatures is a relatively new field of engineering involving new materials, new manufacturing techniques, and new test methods. The knowledge and experience gained during the development and testing of the SST will contribute to this field.

5. *Aircraft Engines*—Realization of SST performance goals requires a significant advance in aircraft engine technology. Performance gains will result largely from operation at significantly higher internal cycle temperatures than have been used commercially in the past. This area of improvement must be accomplished without sacrificing engine life or maintenance characteristics normally associated with airline operations. Advanced noise suppression techniques are required if these advanced engines are to comply with evolving noise standards.

6. *Fuel Tank Sealants*—The high temperature environment of the SST fuel tanks necessitates the development of sealants usable to temperatures of 500° F. These compounds may find broader applicability in other aircraft applications.

7. *Environmental Control System*—The SST environmental control system will require advanced development

of lightweight air compressors, small high-speed turbines, and lightweight, accurate, and reliable system controls.

General Technology

1. *Metals and Alloys*—The SST Program will create a new level of demand for titanium alloys which is expected to accelerate use of this very useful material over a broad spectrum of applications. High engine temperatures will require development of new high-temperature alloys.

2. *Metal Joining Techniques*—New techniques for metal joining are expected to be reduced to manufacturing practice in the SST Program as a result of a need for efficient fabrication operations and in connection with weight reduction. Diffusion bonding is a new metal joining technique which permits high strength joining of complex surfaces without parent metal strength reduction due to heating.

3. *High Temperature Nonmetallic Materials*—The severe high temperature environment of the SST necessitates development of new materials for use in this environment, including glass and lightweight composite structural materials made of plastic binders and boron or carbon fibers.

4. *High Temperature Seals*—The SST will represent the first use of hydrodynamic or hydrostatic seals in aircraft applications.

5. *Hydraulic Fluids and System Components and Lubricants*—Because of the temperatures encountered in the SST and the long life required, new types of fluids, lubricants, and system components must be developed which are expected to have important industrial applications.

6. *Brakes*—The SST Program is responsible for a search for new brake materials with improved heat-sink characteristics. These materials when developed would be broadly applicable to many different types of vehicles.

7. *Electrical System Components*—The high temperatures encountered by the SST require advanced development of wire insulation, antenna parts, and electrical system components capable of withstanding this severe environment.

Question 2: What value or importance do these technologies have to our national research and development posture?

It has been suggested that the technological benefits from the SST program are impressive enough in themselves to provide strong justification for SST prototype development. It is our view that this statement unduly magnifies the significance and impact of the advances which will inevitably result from a high technology program such as the SST. Although past experience has in many cases demonstrated that predictions of technological fallout can be extraordinarily conservative when projected over a number of years into the future, we nevertheless find claims for technological fallout from the SST Program to be generally unconvincing. Many of the technologies are refinements of developments which had their origin in DoD or other aircraft programs. Others appear to be of such a highly specialized character that broader application to other areas of the economy are limited, and in any event many years from being realized.

What then is the contribution of the SST Program to our national research and development posture? It would appear to occur in two principal ways: manpower, challenge.

The Boeing Company has estimated that the design and prototype phase of the SST Program will require a peak level employment of approximately 20,000 people, of which 3,400 are expected to be skilled engineers and technical personnel. This is about 7% of the peak level employment in support of the Apollo program. As in the case of Apollo, but to a lesser degree, the SST Program, therefore, will both drain and stimulate the technical manpower pool in the U.S. We are not capable of judging the net positive or negative values in this area. For example, in the limited time available for this effort, it has not been possible to project other major programs into the same time period to determine whether the manpower drain will be at the expense of programs of potentially greater return. We have also not been able to judge the degree of stimulation to the training of future aeronautical engineers vital to the nation which may result from the existence of a visible and challenging SST development program. We expect in any event that the most significant effect will, in fact, result from the second factor—challenge.

The SST Program can provide considerable, but unmeasurable benefit because of the challenge, both in a technical and emotional sense which such a competitive and forward-looking program engenders. This sense of challenge, particularly if successfully met, can be a beneficial factor not only in the aircraft industry but also on a broader basis and on a national level.

In addition the technical challenge of a specific program can serve as a useful focus for research and technology programs and may thereby force new and important breakthroughs.

Question 3: What are the national security implications of technologies advanced by the SST Program? Are they unique to the SST or will other programs provide similar benefits?

The question of whether the SST advances will have national security implications is relatively easy to answer. Of course defense capabilities will be enhanced by the technology advances made by the SST. What value can be placed on these benefits, however, is *much more* difficult to answer.

Both civil and military aircraft performance and efficiency are dependent upon the achievement of such factors as strong, lightweight structures, low aerodynamic drag and high thrust-to-weight engines with low fuel consumption. The SST Program is directed toward achieving gains in these areas. To the extent the SST Program is successful, there will undoubtedly be application of these results to help provide better military systems. In general, however, the technology rather than particular systems can be expected to be transferred to military use, because of different systems requirements.

In many areas, this technology interchange takes place from the military program to the SST. For example, in titanium technology, the military have pioneered the use of this material for aircraft structures, such as the rear portion of the P-8 fighter, and the YF-12 and SR-71. The processing and manufacturing techniques being developed for the SST have their origin with these aircraft. Similarly, the two new fighter aircraft programs being initiated, the F-14 and F-15, while of relatively lower performance than the SST and therefore not requiring titanium for its high temperature qualities, will nevertheless be ⅓ to ½ titanium by weight and will employ the latest design and fabrication techniques. These aircraft will have their first flights before the SST so this technology will be proceeding on a parallel basis.

Similarly, there are military programs directed to developing better and lighter materials, for advanced engines, more efficient cooling and design features to increase aircraft engine temperatures, just as is being done in the SST. For example, DoD has a program to develop new technology engines for the F–14 and F–15 that are more advanced technologically than the SST engine. These developments are essentially parallel to the SST engine program, and are drawing from the same data base. Similarly the Advanced Manned Strategic Aircraft (AMSA) engine, even more advanced and coming in a later time period, will utilize the advances of both programs.

Another development that has been indicated as mutually beneficial is the fly-by-wire control systems being developed for the SST. Similar systems are being developed for military aircraft. Both systems are directed at the same objective, the substitution of electrical connections between the pilot and the controls for the present mechanical connections. Weight savings, better reliability and less susceptibility to enemy gun fire provide significant military advantages.

These are only a few of the many examples that can be cited of mutual interaction between the SST and military aircraft programs, in which each program benefits from the other. Specific applications are somewhat different in each area however, warranting separate approaches even though technology and principles are the same. Alternative approaches also provide the opportunity of developing new solutions to fundamental problems as a result of addressing these problems on multiple fronts.

In summary, the technologies advanced by the SST Program will contribute to advancement in military weapons systems but military systems will not depend in a substantive way upon the SST for such improvements. The SST Program cannot be considered as providing unique technological inputs to military programs.

Letters by Dr. Lee A. DuBridge, National Science Adviser

THE WHITE HOUSE,
Washington, March 20, 1969.

Memorandum for Hon. James M. Beggs, Chairman, SST Ad Hoc Review Committee.

Subject: Committee Report.

In response to your memorandum of March 19, 1969, I have reviewed the draft report of the ad hoc Committee. It is my view that the report in its present form is not acceptable since it does not adequately reflect the range of uncertainties and general negative character of the panel reports and committee discussions as I understand them.

I am preparing detailed comments and suggestions for modifications to the report and will forward them to you as soon as they are available.

LEE A. DUBRIDGE,
Science Adviser

———

EXECUTIVE OFFICE OF THE PRESIDENT, OFFICE OF SCIENCE AND TECHNOLOGY,
Washington, D.C., March 20, 1969.

Hon. JAMES M. BEGGS,
Under Secretary, Department of Transportation, Washington, D.C.

DEAR MR. BEGGS: This is in response to your invitation to make any recommendation on the SST question.

I do not feel I should file a formal recommendation at this point, but I would like to make informal comments to you.

The subject of SST has been under review by members of the President's Science Advisory Committee and by the staff of OST for several years. We have recently been going over the current reports and had a thorough briefing from the Boeing representatives last week. My own conclusions are as follows:

1. The SST is probably technologically feasible, but the very small ratio of payload to total weight is so small that unexpected problems during the development could greatly reduce that payload and make the airplane commercially

unattractive. There are enough unsolved technological problems that it is risky to make specific assumptions as to what the payload will be. It may turn out to be somewhat larger or somewhat smaller than now estimated. Thus, this is still a high risk question.

2. I have been impressed by the statements which have been made about the doubtful commercial viability of an SST. I conclude that previous estimates have possibly been over optimistic as to the number of planes which would be sold, as to the price at which they could be sold (if there were no government subsidy) and whether this would have a positive or negative effect on our balance of payments. If one makes pessimistic assumptions, though still reasonable ones, it could turn out that the plane is not commercially attractive to the airlines in sufficient numbers to make it profitable either for the manufacturer or for airline operators.

3. The noise problem is still a matter for worry. Although it appears that the noise on approach and takeoff will be reasonable, the noise radiated sideways is still very high and there seems at present to be no assured way in which this noise can be reduced to acceptable levels. In addition, it is very likely that noise standards will change during the next eight years as residents in airport areas become more sensitive to the problem. If current noise standards cannot be met, it would seem to be difficult even with new technological inventions to meet future more stringent noise requirements.

4. The sonic boom problem is, of course, quite unsolved, and even at best will cause enormous public concern. Surely we must have a policy statement that there shall be no supersonic operations by the SST over any populated areas.

5. Closely related to the problem of the payload is the problem of the maximum range of the aircraft. At present this is marginal for long overseas flights, and it is not clear whether further development efforts will cause the range to increase or decrease. Past history suggests a hopeful point of view, but this cannot be assured.

6. The competition of French and Russian SST's seems to be far less serious than we thought a couple of years ago.

On the whole, I come out negative on the desirability for further government subsidy for the development of this plane and would suggest that the possibility be explored of turning the remainder of the development and, of course, all of the production expenditures over to private enterprise. Any technological benefits which would accrue from its further development, either for civilian or military purposes, would seem to be minimal.

Granted that this is an exciting technological development, it still seems best to me to avoid the serious environmental and nuisance problems and the Government should not be subsidizing a device which has neither commercial attractiveness nor public acceptance.

> Sincerely,
>
> LEE A. DUBRIDGE,
>
> *Director.*

Letter by Honorable Russell Train,
Undersecretary of the Interior

> U.S. DEPARTMENT OF THE INTERIOR,
> *Washington, D.C., March 21, 1969.*

Memorandum to Chairman, SST Ad Hoc Review Committee (Under Secretary Beggs).

From Under Secretary of the Interior.
Subject SST Ad Hoc Review Committee Report.

I have reviewed the above draft report, and my comments are submitted herewith.

Having listened to the reports of the subcommittees on March 12 and the discussion which followed each report, I was struck by the lack of positive justification for the SST program.

1. While the Balance of Payments Working Panel report indicated that there is evidence that a favorable balance might result from sales of aircraft and parts, it was strongly indicated that there is no positive evidence of balance of payment benefit when all aspects of the matter, including increased U.S. travel abroad, are taken into account.

2. The representative of the Council of Economic Advisers expressed an opinion that the estimates of aircraft sales are quite arbitrary. This would bear upon Point 1 above.

3. I believe that your draft report attaches more significance to technology fall-out from the program than does the actual report of that subcommittee. The latter stated "the magnitude of this effect is very difficult to assess, *but it appears to be small*." (Emphasis supplied.) The subcommittee goes on to say "We believe technological fall-out to be of relatively minor importance in this program and therefore should not be considered either wholly or in part as a basis for justifying the program." On the relation of technological fall-out to defense programs, the subcommittee concluded: "The SST program cannot be considered as providing unique, technological inputs to military programs." My own notes of the discussion indicate that DOD does not expect significant military application of SST.

4. The Economic Subcommittee emphasized the "uncertainty" connected with the program. The subcommittee concluded that: "Probably the single most uncertain aspect of the whole program relates to the uncertainty as to whether an SST can be built in the given time that will meet the specifications of being efficient, safe, and economical."

5. The Environmental and Sociological Subcommittee pointed to significant potential environmental and sociological problems related to the health and well-being of the people which must be considered in making decisions concerning the SST. The principal problem areas were identified as: (1) sonic boom; (2) airport noise, (3) hazards to passengers and crew; and (4) effects of water vapor in the atmosphere. I would add pollution resulting from engine discharges as an additional significant environmental problem. It is my understanding that operation at subsonic speeds, including speeds necessary for takeoff and landing, results in inefficient fuel combustion with a resulting heavy discharge of pollutants into the atmosphere. Both atmospheric pollution and ground contamination seem likely to result.

On the subject of research, it was indicated that far more research is needed with respect to:

a. Engine noise and noise suppressants;
b. Electrical control and guidance systems;
c. Market research.

On the basis of the above record, it is my own conclusion

that the justification for proceeding with the program is not now apparent. There may be other considerations with which I am not familiar. The Department of the Interior has no special capability for evaluating such matters as the technological fall-out resulting from the program or its implications for balance of payments. However, we consider the environmental disadvantages to be of extreme significance. The growing environmental deterioration in this country and abroad is already the cause of widespread public concern. We believe that the probable adverse environmental impact of the SST is such that the program should not be pursued in the absence of overwhelming evidence of positive advantages.

In the meantime, the Department would urge and support continuing research directed to eliminating or reducing to reasonable levels adverse environmental impacts.

RUSSELL E. TRAIN.

**Letter by Dr. Charles C. Johnson, Jr.,
Assistant Surgeon General Administrator**

DEPARTMENT OF HEALTH, EDUCATION, AND WELFARE, PUBLIC HEALTH SERVICE, CONSUMER PROTECTION AND ENVIRONMENTAL HEALTH SERVICE,

Washington, D.C., March 20, 1969.

HON. JAMES M. BEGGS,
Under Secretary of Transportation,
Washington, D.C.

DEAR MR. BEGGS: The Environmental and Sociological Panel shares the view expressed in your memorandum of March 19, 1969, to the effect that "this Committee's views must be clearly and fully presented to the Secretary, he in turn to utilize them and incorporate them in his report to the President."

We are very concerned, therefore, that the summary of our report attached to your memorandum does not clearly and fully present our views. It appears to represent a synopsis of an oral presentation given in lieu of a specific reading of the report contents at a meeting of the Committee. As such, the summary report does not convey the real sense of the Environmental and Sociological Panel's report and does not adequately reflect its concerns. On the contrary, the editorial comments, interpretations and implied conclusions in the draft summary tend to convey the impression that the panel considered the environmental factors to be of small moment. Quite to the contrary these must be recognized as being of significant concern and emphasized at every step leading to a final decision in this matter.

Our understanding concerning the development of collective views and the presentation of recommendations were submitted in our previous letter. The attached summary presents the views of the Environmental and Sociological Panel more precisely and within the approximate space you have allotted to this subject. It is requested that this summary be substituted for the version attached to your memorandum of March 19.

Sincerely yours,

CHARLES C. JOHNSON, JR.
Assistant Surgeon General Administrator.

———

SUMMARY OF REPORT OF THE ENVIRONMENTAL AND SOCIOLOGICAL PANEL OF THE AD HOC SUPERSONIC TRANSPORT REVIEW COMMITTEE, MARCH 20, 1969

ENVIRONMENTAL AND SOCIOLOGICAL IMPACT

The Panel considers the principal environmental and sociological problem areas to be: (1) Sonic boom; (2) Airport noise; (3) Hazards to passengers and crew; and (4) Effects of water vapor in the atmosphere.

The effects of sonic boom are such as to be considered intolerable by a very high percentage of the people affected. The Panel is very concerned about the economic pressures that will be exerted if it is subsequently found that the economic success of the aircraft depends on overland flights at supersonic speeds. The Panel believes it is essential that the public be formally assured by appropriate authorities that commercial supersonic flight over land will not be permitted.

"The development of methods to reduce engine noise is an essential element in the development of the SST as well as subsonic jet aircraft. Reduction of engine noise, however, is more difficult for the SST. These engines are fundamentally noisier than the fan engines that are optimum for the subsonic jets." (The SST Program and Related National Benefits, Feb. 17, 1969, the Boeing Company, page 6-22.)

On the ground the SST is significantly noisier than the 707. On landing and takeoff the SST can be expected to produce noise levels exceeding 100 PNdB directly under the plane over a distance of 13 miles. Surrounding the runway an area 4 miles long and approximately 2 miles wide would be exposed to noise levels in excess of 100 PNdB. It can be expected that significant numbers of residents will file complaints and resort to legal action, and that a very high percentage of the exposed population will find the noise intolerable and the apparent cause of a wide variety of adverse effects. Land use planning in the vicinity of airports is the only satisfactory solution to this problem at the present time. Airport personnel and airline passengers, however, will be exposed to very high noise levels regardless of land use planning. Prolonged exposure to intense noise produces permanent hearing loss and may also disrupt job performance by interfering with speech communication, distracting attention, and otherwise complicating the demands of the task. Noise-induced hearing loss looms as a major health hazard in American industry. However, a national hearing conservation standard governing allowable or safe exposures remains to be established.

SST crews and passengers are incomparably more dependent on the proper functioning of equipment for pressurization, temperature control, and oxygen systems than are the occupants of subsonic aircraft. A loss of pressure at 65,000 feet would result in all aboard losing consciousness within fifteen seconds. At cruise altitudes ozone is present in concentrations which would be highly toxic to passengers if allowed to enter the plane. The radiation hazard would be approximately 100 times greater than at ground level. SST crews probably should be placed in the category of radiation workers and kept under close surveillance.

The widespread use of supersonic transports will introduce large quantities of water vapor into the stratosphere which could alter the radiation balance and thereby possibly affect the general circulation of atmospheric components.

Letter by Honorable Arnold Weber,
Assistant Secretary of Labor

U.S. DEPARTMENT OF LABOR,
Washington, D.C., March 26, 1969.

Hon. JAMES M. BEGGS,
Under Secretary, Department of Transportation,
Washington, D.C.

DEAR MR. BEGGS: As agreed at yesterday's meeting of
the Ad Hoc Committee, this letter supersedes my letter of
March 21. It is my understanding that the report of the
Ad Hoc Review Committee on the SST will be made up
of (a) the reports of the four working panels and (b) this
and letters from other Committee members setting forth
additional views and recommendations.

I wish to summarize for the record the oral comments
which I made yesterday to Secretary Volpe as follows:

1. The range of uncertainty with respect to the economic
benefits from the SST is such that no clear case can be
made on economic grounds for proceeding with the SST
development.

2. Technological spill over benefits appear to be negligible.

3. There are major environmental and social problems
which have not been solved and which should be the subject of further intensive research before proceeding with
prototype construction.

4. The effect of SST development on the balance of
payments is likely to be negative because of the probable
major increase in United States tourism abroad.

5. The net employment increase from SST production
would likely be negligible and would occur in the professional and technical categories where shortages already
exist. The project would have practically no employment
benefits for the disadvantaged hard-core unemployed with
low skill levels.

In addition, we would recommend that the responsibility
for long term research and development activities related
to supersonic flight should be shifted from the Federal
Aviation Agency of the Department of Transportation to
the National Aeronautics and Space Administration. The

Bibliography

A-1 Acoustical Society of America, "Proceedings of the Sonic Boom Symposium," *Journal of the Acoustical Society of America*, No. 39, May 1966, 80 pages.

A-2 *Aerospace Technology*, May 20, 1968. Comprehensive account of the 1967 design of Boeing SST.

A-3 American Speech and Hearing Association, *Proceedings* of the June 13-14, 1968, Washington, D.C. National Conference on "Noise as a Public Health Hazard."

A-4 Anti-Concorde Project, miscellaneous newsletters, pamphlets, leaflets, etc., published by R. Wiggs, 70 Lytton Avenue, Letchworth, Herts, England.

A-5 *Aviation Week and Space Technology*, October 28, 1968, "Structure Critical for SST" and "Eurocontrol Readies Procedures for SST."

B-1 Baker, L., *The Guaranteed Society*, Macmillan, New York (1968), 276 pages.

B-2 Bauer, R. A., "Some Thoughts on Human Response to Sonic Boom," talk given at October 22, 1968 meeting of American Institute of Aeronautics and Astronautics, in Philadelphia.

B-3 Baxter, W. F., "The SST: From Watts to Harlem in Two Hours," *Stanford Law Review*, November 1968, pp. 1-57. Superb exposition of the physics of the sonic boom and the legal problems created by widespread damage to buildings and annoyance to people.

B-4 Bentley, B. M., "The Sonic Boom," New England Research Center, University of Connecticut, Storrs, Connecticut. A collection of excellent papers of several years ago.

B-5 Bolt, Beranek, and Newman, Inc., "Laboratory Tests of Subjective Reactions to Sonic Booms," by K. S. Pearsons and K. D. Kryter. Report NASA-CR-187, March 1965.

B-6 Booz, Allen, and Hamilton, Inc., "Supersonic Transport Financial Planning Study," FAA Contract FA-SS-66-23; AD 652314; May 16, 1967, 350 pages.

B-7 Boring, E. G., H. S. Langfeld, and H. P. Weld, "Foundations of Psychology," Wiley, 1948.

B-8   Borsky, P. N., National Opinion Research Center Report 101, Part 2, 1965. AMRL-TR-65-37, Vol. II, AD-625332.

B-9   Brisson (Medecin-Lt. Col. de Brisson), "Etude d'opinion sur le bang supersonique," Libr. Trans. 1159, Royal Aircraft Establishment. Says 35% of French citizens interrogated said they "definitely could not" tolerate ten booms a day.

B-10   British Aircraft Corporation, "Concorde," an 8-page newspaper-size brochure of 1968.

C-1   Carlson, H. W. and F. E. McLean, "The Sonic Boom," *International Science & Technology, 55,* July 1966.

C-2   Caso, R. G., "Town of Hempstead News," October 8, 1968, and October 9, 1968 statement presented to the FAA, pages 2 & 5.

C-3   Chacona, C. J., "The High and the Mighty: the SST Charivari," Thesis, Harvard University, 1968, 35 pages.

C-4   Citizens League Against the Sonic Boom (C.L.A.S.B.), Fact-Sheet 10, March 1968.

C-5   C.L.A.S.B., Fact-Sheet 11b, February 1968.

C-6   C.L.A.S.B., Fact-Sheet 15, May 1968.

C-7   C.L.A.S.B., "SST and Sonic Boom Handbook," 5th edition, October 15, 1969, 80 pages.

D-1   Dwiggins, D., "The SST: Here It Comes, Ready or Not," Doubleday, New York (1969), 294 pages.

E-1   Edwards, C. B., "Concorde, a Study in Cost-Benefit Analysis," Economics Department, University of East Anglia, 17 pages. Available through Anti-Concorde Project.

G-1   General Electric Company brochure AEG-240R-6/68 (10M).

G-2   Gleason, G. K., "The Supersonic Transport and the Boom Problem," Thesis for Harvard Law School Seminar on Legal Protection of Environmental Quality, May 31, 1968, 166 pages.

G-3   Graves, C. Edward, "Sonic Booms and Wilderness," *The Living Wilderness,* No. 99, Winter 1967-68.

H-1   Harris, H. I., "Assault on Emotional Health," *American Journal of Psychiatry 125,* 3 September 1968, page 159.

H-2   Huard, L. A., "The Roar, The Whine, The Boom and The Law: Some Legal Concerns about the SST," *Santa Clara Lawyer,* Spring 1969, 37 pages.

I-1   Institute for Defense Analyses, Inc., "Economic Effects of the Sonic Boom," N. J. Asher, *et al,* December 1964, AD 655608, 144 pages.

I-2   Institute for Defense Analyses, Inc., "Demand Analysis for Air Travel by Supersonic Transport," Report R-118, December 1966, two volumes, AD-652309 and AD-652310. Indicates that perhaps 100 to 200 Boeing SSTs would be sold if overland supersonic flight were forbidden.

I-3   International Commission on Radiological Protection, Task Group on the Biological Effects of High-Energy Radiation, "Radiobiological Aspects of the Supersonic Transport," *Health Physics 12,* 209-226 (1966). Detailed analysis of cosmic ray problem.

J-1   John A. Blume and Associates Research Division, "Response of Structures to Sonic Booms Produced by XB-70, B-58 and F-104 Aircraft," J. A. Blume, *et al.,* Report 662003 of October 1967. Prepared for National Sonic Boom Evaluation Office.

K-1   Kryter, K. D., "Sonic Booms from Supersonic Transport," *Science* January 24, 1969, page 359.

L-1   Landis, C., and W. A. Hunt, "The Startle Reaction," Farrar and Rinehart, 1939.

L-2   Lardner, G. Jr., "Supersonic Scandal," *New Republic,* March 16, 1968.

L-3   Library of Congress, "Policy Planning for Aeronautical Research and Development," Document 90, 89th Congress, 2nd Session. May 19, 1966, 280 pages.

L-4   *Liverpool Journal of Commerce,* December 11, 1967.

L-5   Lundberg, B., "Speed and Safety in Civil Aviation," Aeronautical Research Institute of Sweden, Report FFA 94, Part I (Speed) and Part II (Safety), 1963.

L-6   Lundberg, B., "Pros and Cons of Supersonic Aviation in Relation to Gains or Losses in the Combined Time-Comfort Consideration," *Journal of Royal Aeronautical Society 68,* September 1964.

L-7   Lundberg, B., "Aviation Safety and the SST," *Astronautics & Aeronautics,* January 1965.

L-8   Lundberg, B., "Supersonic Aviation, a Testcase for Democracy," NATO's Fifteen Nations, April-July 1965 issues.

L-9   Lundberg, B., "The Menace of the Sonic Boom to Society and Civil Aviation," Aeronautical Research Institute of Sweden, Report FFA-PE-19, May 1966.

L-10   Lundberg, B., "Atmospheric Magnification of Sonic Booms in the Oklahoma Tests," Aeronautical Research Institute of Sweden, Report 112 of June 1967.

L-11   Lundberg, B., "The Uneconomic Unwanted SST," August 15, 1967, 44 pages.

L-12   Lundberg, B., "Observations Regarding the Acceptable Nominal Sonic Boom Overpressure in SST Operation Over Land," August 30, 1968.

L-13   Lundberg, B., "Observations Regarding the Sonic Boom in SST Operation Over Sea," BL Report 109-A of September 16, 1968.

L-14   Lundberg, B., "Acceptable Nominal Sonic Boom Overpressure in SST Operation Over Land and Sea," paper presented at June 14, 1968 National Conference on Noise as a Public Health Hazard, American Speech & Hearing Association.

L-15   Lundberg, B., "Implications and Justification of the SST," from "The Sonic Boom," a 2 October 1968 symposium, Nederlands Akoestisch Genootschap, Delft, Netherlands. Postbus 162, Publication No. 15, April 1969, pages 33-69.

L-16   Lundberg, B., "Summary Statement on the Unacceptability of the SST Sonic Boom Over Land and Sea and the Economic Losses of SST Operation Confined to Oversea Routes," BL Report 118, October 24, 1969, 16 pages.

M-1   Mohler, S. R., "Ionizing Radiation and the SST," *Astronautics & Aeronautics,* September 1964.

M-2   Murphy, C. J. V., "Boeing's Ordeal with the SST," *Fortune,* October 1968, page 129.

N-1   National Academy of Sciences, Committee on SST-Sonic Boom, "Generation and Propagation of Sonic Boom," October 1967.

N-2   National Academy of Sciences, Committee on SST-Sonic Boom, "Physical Effects of the Sonic Boom," February 1968.

N-3   National Academy of Sciences, Committee on SST-Sonic Boom, "Human Responses to the Sonic Boom," June 1968.

N-4   National Academy of Sciences, Clarifying material called "Statement of the Committee on SST-Sonic Boom," August 19, 1968; prepared in response to C.L.A.S.B. request that a false conclusion in an earlier report be corrected.

N-5   National Sonic Boom Evaluation Office Report NSBEO-1-67, "Sonic Boom Experiments at Edwards Air Force Base," Interim Report 28 July 1967.

N-6   Newberry, C. S., "Response of Buildings to Sonic Booms," *Journal of Sound and Vibration 6,* 406 (1967).

O-1   Organisation for Economic Cooperation and Develop-
       ment, Directorate for Scientific Affairs: "The Sonic
       Boom and Its Implications for Public Policy," by the
       Secretariat, DAS/CSI/T/69.53, 53 pages, 20 June
       1969. Also "Report in Five Parts on the Sonic Boom,"
       prepared in August 1969 by G. M. Lilley for OECD
       Conference on the Sonic Boom, 270 pages.

P-1   Pao, Y. H. and A. Goldburg, "Clear Air Turbulence,"
       Consultants Bureau, New York, New York, 1969.
P-2   Parent, M., "Effects des vols supersoniques," 17-page
       article in *Les Monuments Historiques de la France,*
       XIV (1968), pages 5-21. Detailed account of sonic-
       boom damage to historic buildings. Illustrated.
P-3   Parkhurst, F. S. Jr., "Noise, Jets, and the Sonic Boom,"
       August 11, 1967, Guilford College, Greensboro, North
       Carolina. A thorough review with excellent bibliogra-
       phy.
P-4   President's SST ad hoc Review Committee, Report of
       March 1969. *Congressional Record,* October 31, 1969,
       pp. H-10432-H-10446. A majority of the members,
       representing twelve agencies of the U.S. Government,
       expressed opposition to the proposed Boeing SST pro-
       gram.

R-1   Ruppenthal, K. M. "The Supersonic Transport: Billion-
       Dollar Dilemma," *Nation,* May 22, 1967 and May 29,
       1967.

S-1   Stanford Research Institute "Sonic Boom Experiments at
       Edwards Air Force Base," 28 July 1967. Report ETU-
       6065. About 300 pages. Issued by National Sonic
       Boom Evaluation Office, 1400 Wilson Boulevard,
       Arlington, Virginia.
S-2   Stanford Research Institute Report "Preliminary Study
       of the Awakening and Startle Effects of Simulated
       Sonic Booms," J. S. Lukas and K. D. Kryter, April
       1968, contract NAS-1-6193.

U-1   U.S. Air Force booklet "Sonic Boom Background Infor-
       mation," 68-1, 1968. Explains that sonic booms from
       supersonic military planes can damage property and
       annoy people, and that an effort is made to minimize
       such flights.
U-2   U.S. Army Human Engineering Laboratories, "Criteria
       for Assessing Hearing Damage Risk from Impulse-
       Noise Exposure," Technical Memorandum 13-67 (AD-
       666206), August, 1967. Comprehensive review of
       studies made here and abroad.

U-3   U.S. Congress, *Hearings,* Department of Transportation Appropriations for 1968, 1024 pages.

U-4   U.S. Congress, *Congressional Record* June 10, 1968, pp. H-4733-4790 (Monumental issue on sonic boom).

U-5   U.S. Congress, *Hearings,* Department of Transportation and Related Agencies Appropriations for 1970. 354 pages.

U-6   U.S. Congress, *Congressional Record* November 18, 1969, pp. H-10995-11032.

U-7   U.S. Department of Agriculture Report, "Effects of Simulated Sonic Booms on Reproduction and Behavior of Farm-Raised Mink," ARS-44-200, June 1968.

U-8   U.S. Department of Justice, letter of April 1, 1968, by E. L. Weisl, Jr., on damage payments in Oklahoma City and elsewhere.

U-9   U.S. Department of the Interior, Sonic Boom Study Group: "Noise and Sonic Boom in Relation to Man," November 4, 1968, 52 pages.

U-10 U.S. Department of Transportation, FAA Report "Final Program Summary: Oklahoma City Sonic Boom Study," Rpt. SST-65-3, March 21, 1965. AD459601.

U-11 U.S. Department of Transportation, Federal Aviation Administration, "U.S. Supersonic Transport: Economic Feasibility Report," April 1967. Approximately 200 pages.

U-12 U.S. Federal Aviation Agency "United States Supersonic Transport Program," Report SST-65-10, July 1965, 44 pp. A chronology.

U-13 U.S. Federal Aviation Administration "Tentative Airworthiness Standards for Supersonic Transports," Revised Ed., Jan. 1, 1969. 207 pp.

U-14 U.S. National Aeronautics and Space Administration Report "Result of USAF-NASA-FAA Flight Program to Study Community Response to Sonic Booms in the Greater St. Louis Area," C. W. Nixon and H. H. Hubbard, NASA TN-D-2705, May 1965.

U-15 U.S. National Aeronautics and Space Administration Report "Sonic Boom Measurements During Bomber Training Operations in the Chicago Area," D. A. Hilton, V. Huckel and D. J. Maglieri, NASA TN-D-3655, October 1966.

U-16 U.S. National Aeronautics and Space Administration, NASA Sp-147, April 12, 1967, 118 pages. A collection of highly technical papers on the sonic boom.

U-17 U.S. National Aeronautics and Space Administration Report "On Supersonic Vehicle Shapes for Reducing Auditory Response to Sonic Booms," W. L. Howes, NASA-TMX-52294, April 12, 1967.

U-18   U.S. National Aeronautics and Space Administration "Second Conference on Sonic Boom Research," NASA Sp-180. May 9-10, 1968.

U-19   U.S. Tenth Circuit Court of Appeals, decision of March 8, 1969, in favor of Oklahoma City homeowners whose claims amounted to $93,705.93.

W-1   World Meteorological Organization, Technical Note No. 89, "Meteorological Problems in the Design and Operation of Supersonic Aircraft" (1967).

Z-1   Zimmerman, F. L. "Supersonic Snow Job," Wall Street Journal, February 9, 1967.

Index